AS HE CAME INTO CAMP HE WAS A PICTURE. PAGE 149.

CAMP FIRE STORIES

A SERIES OF SKETCHES OF THE

UNION ARMY IN THE SOUTHWEST

BY

EDWARD ANDERSON,

COLONEL 12TH INDIANA VOLUNTEER CAVALRY,
PAST CHAPLAIN IN CHIEF G. A. R.

ILLUSTRATED.

CHICAGO:
STAR PUBLISHING COMPANY

DEDICATION.

To the memory of "The Little Mother" this volume is affectionately dedicated by her husband.

PREFACE.

Somehow a story seems to tell what war meant, in all its phases, better than does a mere description; and what a man has seen and felt is better understood if the incidents of the seeing and feeling are graphically told by the one who did them both.

So I have yielded as "the boys" have urged that I write these stories out as they have been told at our Grand Army Camp-Fires; because, they said, we old soldiers would be soon dead, and the young folks who had grown up to take our places should have left them our legacy of experience—the fun and the pathos, the drama and the tragedy—that they might know what their fathers went through in saving this country during its first internecine strife.

Therefore I have written these Camp-Fire stories for the old comrades in arms to the reviving of their memories, and for their sons and daughters to the letting them see what war was. Five of the hospital stories were published a few years ago in the "Golden Rule," the organ of the Y. P. S. C. E., though even these are retold in this book; two or three have been published in local papers; and at least two of the jokes I gave to Harper's Drawer.

No one can know what help I have had in this from

the lovely daughter who has been at my elbow all the way through the writing of these stories; with a jog to memory here, and a righting up of some incident there, as she got them from her heroic but now sainted mother, who was closely identified with the war and whose blessed ministrations more than one soldier can call to mind.

So I send out my book of stories and their pictures by pen and pencil, and hope it may make many an eye that grows rheumy with age flash out again the old fires of years ago, and many a young face light up with a new-born patriotism and a fresh sense of the grand blood which is of heroes and which flows in the veins of these young people, and will help fire them up for the securing of a better country to hand down to their children than even their fathers saved and gave to them.

CONTENTS.

	Page.
1. The French Colonel	1
2. The Hospital Sheet	6
3. Tim Hickey and the Donkey	12
4. Irish Wit	18
5. Tim Hickey and the Flag	24
6. Raw Officers	30
7. The Devoted Major	36
8. The Sharpshooters	42
9. Boys	47
10. The Bugler	52
11. Jingle	58
12. Little Wes	63
13. Big Wes	68
14. Discomforts	74
15. Aunt Ev.	82
16. Forrest and the Silver Pistol	87
17. Colonel Dick Mather's Leap	93
18. Pocahontas	98
19. Bravery	133
20. Quantrell	139
21. Caught Again	145
22. The Sabre Test	151
23. The New Generation	156
24. Sigel	160
25. Sigel II	166
26. Colonel Nageley's Brevet	173
27. Bummers	179

CONTENTS.

28. Captain Phil. Ritchie's Ride 185
29. Cannon Balls 191
30. Impressive Services 195
31. Jack Boswell 199
32. Courage in Battle 204
33. The Hospital Hymn 210
34. Muleteers 217
35. Little Piety 223
36. The Hospital Nurse 233
37. You'll Be Sorry for It Some Day 239
38. The Southern Dominie 245
39. The Northern Chaplain 250
40. The Pay of Glory 255

FULL PAGE ILLUSTRATIONS.

	Page.
As he came into camp he was a picture	Frontispiece
"By ——, zat was me"	4
Tim was a sort of a Mark Tapley	13
"Here's me and me horse"	16
"And me wid me hat on"	21
They got him gently from the field	27
"Get into rows, get into rows"	33
"Colonel, the sharpshooters are firing at your fur cap"	43
Taking off his shoe he showed me a card	50
Leading a cake walk dance was Wes in my best uniform	65
Big Wes	69
He gloated over the "Northern Mudsills"	76
He had been a cook in Paris	78
"I've looked at you often enough through a field glass"	89
They spent an evening in delightful reminiscence	91
Old Parchment	98
She was drinking in the deep bass of his voice	105
"Who goes there?" cried the sentry	116
Pocahontas nursing the Major	130
The Captain stood leaning against a tree whittling a bit of stick	137
Bushwhackers waiting for the enemy	140
The bummer's return to camp	180
When bumming was made a legitimate part of war	184
"I've got you spotted"	188
A lady with a little basket on her arm came into the ward	201
Little Piety	223
"I thank God for Little Piety"	231
He had saved the life of the officer	241
We sat together in my study	257
It was a letter telling of the death of his wife	268
I did remember her	271

CAMP FIRE STORIES.

THE FRENCH COLONEL.

> I thought upon one pair of English legs
> Did march three Frenchmen.
>   —Henry V., Act III., Scene 6.

> Some scruple rose, but thus he eased his thought,
> "I'll now give sixpence where I gave a groat;
> Where once I went to church, I'll now go twice—
> And am so clear, too, of all other vice."—Pope.

E HAD a cavalry colonel who was a Frenchman, and who, though a martinet in discipline, was utterly unable to keep his men within bounds. One day, as another cavalry colonel, who had been a minister before the war, was calling at the headquarters of the general of division, he was asked to stay, as the French colonel had been sent for on account of the depredations of his men. When he came the general said

"I understand it has come to be a by-word all through this region that when the bugles of your regiment sound the chickens run under the barns and hide!"

"Zey say, zat when my bugles sound, ze chickens

"I like you to look at ze regiment commanded by zis —— ministare."

run under ze barns and hide! Hein! I like you to look at ze regiment commanded by zis —— ministare! When ze bugles of his regiment sound ze chickens don't run under ze barns and hide, for zey lie on zair backs and hold up zair legs to be tied!"

Long years after the war was over and all had settled down to peace again our French colonel was called to be professor in one of the most orthodox of colleges. His old comrade in arms came to visit him, and was received with a most enthusiastic welcome, which was as profane as it was effusive; for the old colonel was celebrated for his profanity that was ingenious and original. It used to be said that he could invent and utter more oaths to the square inch than any other trooper a-field. While the ex-colonel and now again reverend gentleman was there, it was proposed that he give the students an evening of army reminiscence, and the professor sat by him on the platform, deeply interested in the stories of olden time, which he often testified by exclamations, and shrugs, and gestures. At last the good doctor told the story of the chickens, though he gave no names, or any clue to his excited comrade who was by him. But as he finished, the professor threw up his hands, and falling back on his old style of speech, cried out:

"By ——! zat was me!"

The effect on the students can be imagined.

While the reverend-colonel was his guest, he said to the professor-colonel:

"How did you, of all men, come to be professor in this old-time orthodox college?"

"Why?"

"Well, you know we have record of your rare profanity. Everybody thought you excelled in that, even for a trooper!"

"Oh, vell!" with a good French shrug, "ven I come

"By —— zat was me."

before ze faculty, zey say zat zey have hear I was in ze habit of usin' ver profane languaze, and I say zat ven. I was in ze armie, I use ze languaze zat ze troops could understand, as ze muleteer does to ze mules; but if zey desire me to come and teach ze young ideas how to shoot, if zey wish it, by ――――, I join ze church."

It is generally supposed that no one can swear like a trooper. I do not know why it is so, for they are grand men, with the hardest service and the most constant, taxing their every nerve. It does not need to be explained, as Shakespeare in "Twelfth Night:" "It comes to pass oft, that a terrible oath, with a swaggering accent sharply twanged off, gives manhood more approbation than ever proof itself would have earned him."

But the idea seems to hold, for when the reverend-colonel was mustered in as chaplain-in-chief to the Grand Army of the Republic, a general who towered even above his tall head, placed his hands on the chaplain's shoulders and said in his deep, rich voice that was heard by all:

"This is a strange thing which I see. A colonel of cavalry made over into a parson, and now mustered in as chaplain-in-chief to the Grand Army of the Republic! What a wonderful facility he must have in theological invective!"

THE HOSPITAL SHEET.

There are certain events which to each man's life are as comets to the earth, seemingly strange, erratic portents; distinct from the ordinary lights which guide our course and mark our seasons, yet true to their own laws, potent in their influences.—Bulwer-Lytton.

Blessed influence of one true loving human soul on another.
George Eliot.

E WERE camped near a little town in the southwest, by the vast springs that form the rarest phase of that section, as they come out of the mountains, broad and deep and blue as the sky that they reflect in their limpid depths; but save their cold, clear water, we had nothing for our men who had been wounded in the recent battle. It was early in the war, and we were far away from the base of what few and imperfect supplies the impoverished government could furnish. We had no sulphate of quinine, no lint or bandages, and, except where surgeons had their own cases of instruments, nothing for the

THE HOSPITAL SHEET.

ghastly, but necessary, operations to be performed. We laid the wounded and sick men on the ground, where a church had been partly built and had been roofed over, but where the floor had not been laid. It was sickening to see them as they lay, dressed in the blue in which they were hurt, and with nothing to do for them but to pour the cold water on their fevered wounds, or to bathe their heads with it, or to let them drink deep and long of it in their parching thirst.

One day, one of the cavalry "bummers" came riding down into camp, shouting, "Christian commission! Christian commission! They're coming! They're coming!"

Sure enough, we saw the two four-mule teams coming down the winding road into the little village and to camp, and it was a glad day to us as we helped to unload. Little iron cots there were, and mattresses, pillows and pillow-slips, sheets and comforters, night shirts and towels, bandages and lint and quinine, canned things, potatoes and onions—who can count up all that came, or tell of the cheers that went up? Those cheers were the soldiers' prayers of thanks, as our doleful miserere was changed to a jubilate that was fairly yelled, and that had a harmony of hearts, if not of voices.

We emptied out a "Secesh Hotel," and turned it into a hospital, and when we had brought into it the men, washed and shaved and combed, they looked comfortable enough, even if only the rough but kind hands of booted and spurred men could attend to them.

One day as the chaplain was going the rounds of the hospital he came upon a room where the man on one of the cots looked at him out of wild, scared eyes. One of his fists was shut up tight, and the corner of the upper sheet was turned in under the blanket.

"I'll keep it as long as I live."

"What makes you look at me so, Bill?" asked the chaplain. "What have you been at? What have you got in your hand?"

"Nothin'," said Bill.

"What have you got the sheet turned down for?" Then, as he pulled it out, and found that a great, jagged hole had been cut in it, he said: "Oh, Bill, were you brought up in a saw-mill, that you cut up a lovely sheet in that way—one that kind and patriotic women have sent us? This isn't any army drawing; it's the Christian commission's. Now look at it!"

"Can't help it," said Bill; "I wouldn't part with it any more than I would with my life."

"Let me see what it is, Bill," said the chaplain. "You needn't be afraid; I won't take it away."

Then, as Bill gave it to him, he read on the piece that had been cut out of the sheet, written in indelible ink, these words:

"Mary Evans, Salem, Mass. God bless the soldier that gets this. I shall pray for him every day."

"The idea," said Bill, "that there's some girl prayin' for me, way off there in Massachusetts, fifteen hundred miles away. Why, I wouldn't give that bit of rag up for no man. I'll keep it as long as I live. And me a cussin' and swearin' trooper, too!"

"I wouldn't part with it, either," said the chaplain.

* * * * * * * * *

The Rev. Dr.—— was sailing up Lake Pepin, where the Mississippi River widens out into one of those most exquisitely beautiful sheets of water that make Minnesota the delight of America. The Maiden's Leap was bright in the western sunshine of the afternoon, and the mountains of Frontenac were shrouding in shadow their foothills that slope down to the glassy

10 CAMP FIRE STORIES.

waters, a very carpet of green. He had been reading, and now was taking in the grandeur of the scene, when a gentleman, who had been walking back and forth near where he sat, stopped before him, and said:

"Do you remember a wounded man who cut a piece out of his sheet in the hospital?"

"I beg your pardon, sir, but were you not chaplain of the ―― regiment of ―― cavalry at ―― in 186―?"

"Yes, sir," said the surprised clergyman; "but why do you ask? Were you there?"

"Do you remember a wounded man who cut a piece out of his sheet in the hospital?"

"Indeed I do," answered the good doctor. "I am not likely to forget that, for I have often told of it."

"I was that man," said the stranger, and he took out his pocket-book, and produced the little piece that he had cut from the sheet more than twenty years before. The cloth was yellow now from time, and the ink dimmed, but the words were perfectly legible. "After the war, chaplain," said he; "I went on to Salem, Mass., to see if I could find that girl; I confess I had some romance in my nature. But she was dead, and people told me she had, clear to the time she died, prayed for her soldier, as she called him, and they took me to the room she had occupied. There, sir, as I saw the chair by which she had offered her pure prayers for me, I said to myself that it was time I began to pray for myself; and there in that room to me so sacred I gave myself to the God whose blessing on me she had so often invoked. I came west again, went through the course of study that is prescribed for a clergyman, and have now been preaching for some years; and I feel she is speaking and working through me as I am at my pastoral work."

The chaplain listened with moistened eyes, and then, pressing the hand of his young brother and old comrade, he said, reverently, "How wonderfully God guides our unknown influences if they are good and honest!"

TIM AND THE DONKEY.

> Cudgel thy brains no more about it, for your dull ass will not mend his pace with beating; and when you are asked this question next, say a grave-maker.—Hamlet, Act V., Scene 1.

IM HICKEY was the pet of the regiment. He was an Irishman, and strong (in more ways than one), and prided himself that he could take a barrel by the chine in his teeth and throw it over his head. But when it came to a whiskey barrel, his teeth were the last things that Tim ever brought into play. Yet he was the pet because he was a sort of Mark Tapley, and came out strong under adverse circumstances. In a long march, under a broiling sun, and when the dust hung heavy about the rear of the column and went along with it, when there was a long way between creeks where the men could drink and fill their canteens; and when the men were tired, or on raw, wet days when even a march couldn't keep the blood warm, then whoever could get up a song with a chorus or make a diversion and a laugh, so that

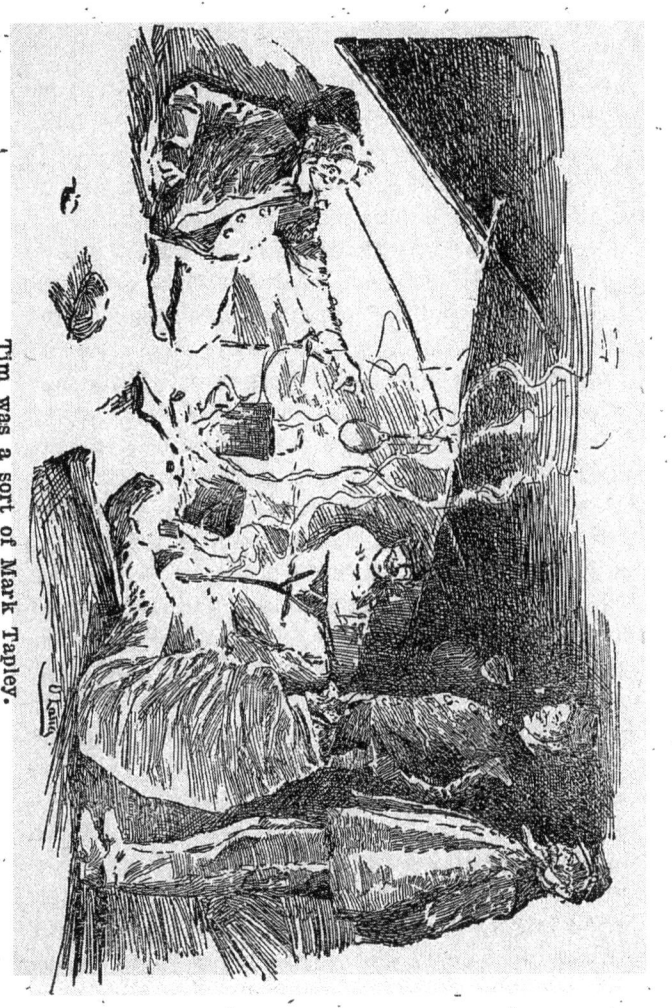

Tim was a sort of Mark Tapley.

the poor fellows would forget their misery for a time and be chirked up for the march to camp or bivouac, was the best fellow in the command.

This Tim always found some new and novel way to do, and both officers and men loved him for it.

One day, in a long, forced march in southwest Missouri, when the dust was thicker than usual and hung like a shroud about the column, while the sun looked like the mouth of a furnace and drove down heat out of a sky of brass, Tim came riding up to me as I was at the rear of the column with a most nondescript rig. He had found somewhere a singularly runty jackass, with the most ponderous ears, the biggest head and the smallest body you can conceive in even a Missouri burro, and with a bridle improvised from a suspender and his gun strap, sat on him, holding up his legs lest they should touch the ground and the donkey trot out from beneath him. In one hand he held his "reins," which he jerked alternately with blows that he gave with a shillalah which he held in the other hand, while his heels were constantly applied to the sides of his beast as though he had spurs. His blue overcoat was his saddle.

As he rode up to me he pulled his foretop with the hand that carried his "whip," and said:

"Might I go forward and schpake to the gineral, sor? I've got business wid him."

"Certainly, Tim," I said. I knew what he was after. It was to cheer up the regiment. So he started with the jerk of the reins, the blow of the stick, which, however, fell on his overcoat and did not hurt the little donkey, and the play of both heels; and the little burro waddled on with no apparent perturbation, while his enormous ears waved back and forth to the time of his miniature legs.

Gen. Jeff. C. Davis was in command of the brigade, and was at the head, and as I rode up on the other side of the column and told him what he had to expect, we could tell how far Tim had come by the roars of the men. Tim kept up a running commentary on his progress with gibes at his "baste," whoops and cat-calls at the men, shouts at the "schpeed of his Bu-cee-phaa-lis," till he reached the general. Looking up in the air at the tall general as he sat on his horse, Tim pulled his forelock again and said:

"Gineral, I've come to ax ye, don't ye need a aid-de-camp" (pronouncing the words as they are spelled). The general, catching the humor of the affair, looked down upon him and said:

"Well, what if I do, Tim?"

"Here's me and me horse!"

The general saw that a new life had come into the men, tired and hot as they were, and he was inclined to keep up the diversion, so he said:

"Tim, you see ahead a bend in the road. Just below there is a stream, and I want you to go and find a good ford."

Tim rode on, with his same equestrian activity, the feet of his little burro keeping to their even cadence and the enormous ears wagging back and forth, and when the column reached the sight of the river Tim was just putting his "horse" into it. Deeper and

"Here's me and me horse."

TIM AND THE DONKEY.

deeper into the water went the little donkey, and higher and higher came Tim's feet to keep them out of it, till he put them between the great ears and he was pivoted on the back of his animal. All at once the burro stepped on a rolling stone and Tim went off into the water. He swam around, caught the donkey by the tail and landed safely on the other side. Then he began to twist the ears of his jackass, and the general called to him:

"What are you doing, Tim?"

"Shure, I'm wringin' out me horse," came back the answer.

Afterward Tim said, as he stood looking at his miniature beast:

"Troth, he's the father of all jack-rabbits!"

IRISH WIT.

In all thy humors, whether grave or mellow,
Thou'rt such a touchy, testy, pleasant fellow,
Hast so much wit and mirth and spleen about thee,
There is no living with thee, or without thee.
      —Addison, Spectator, No. 68.

We grant, although he had much wit,
He was very shy of using it.—Hudibras.

TIM was so reliable (most of the time) that I detailed him as orderly and kept him with me when I had occasion to be away from headquarters on any special duty, and in my rides out for pleasure. One day, in New Orleans, accompanied by several orderlies, of whom Tim was the life and the leader, we came out of St. Charles Street into Canal, where stands the great bronze statue of Henry Clay, into the pedestal of which Gen. Butler had had cut extracts from some of his speeches that must have been specially harassing to the citizens of that city.

Tim rode up alongside me and said:

IRISH WIT.

"Sor, do them paple in Niew Orleans like a nigger so well that they'll put his figger on the best sthreet they've got?"

"That isn't a nigger, Tim," I said, "that's Clay."

"Is that Clay, sor?"

"It's a lie for it's iron."

"Yes, Tim."

"Might I go look at it, sor?"

"Certainly, Tim."

Tim rode over to it, got off his horse and looked it

all about, and then remounting rode back to me with every expression of disgust.

"Did they tell yees that that is Clay, sor?"

"Yes, Tim. Why?"

"It's a lie, sor; it's iron!"

We rode on to Jackson Square, opposite the French Catholic Cathedral, and I ordered Tim to leave the horses with the other orderlies and stroll with me through that beautiful park, with its southern shrubbery and its rare plants that would be exotics with us. Of all his racy comments on the horticultural rarities that were new and amazing to him I cannot recall any of note after all these years. But he walked about among the splendid flowers, inhaled their rich perfumes, and seemed to realize that only the humid airs of the Louisiana Mississippi could produce anything so wonderful. But at last we came upon the colossal statue of General Jackson.

"Who's that, sor, sittin' up upon the horse?" asked Tim.

"That's Jackson, Tim," I said.

"Is that Jackson, sor?"

"Yes, Tim."

Now I don't know as you will believe me when I say it, but Tim, Irishman though he was, was an intense Democrat!

"Is it General Jackson, sor?" he asked, excitedly.

"Yes, Tim."

"The father of dimocracy, sor?" very eagerly.

"Yes, Tim."

"And me wid me hat on!" he cried, snatching it off

"And me wid me hat on," he cried, snatching it off.

and holding it in his hand, as he did all the balance of the time we were in the park.

But Tim had his serious side, as well. I recollect one day I was walking along the levee at Carrollton, just above New Orleans, and Tim was with me. The river laps almost the edge of the levee, while on the land side there must be a slope of ten or twelve feet at least. On the land side we saw every now and then little streaks of wet, as though the water was percolating through the bank. Tim saw them, got down the levee to feel of them and make sure they were wet, and then asked:

"How does them sthreaks of wet come in the le-vee, sor, and not git the whole bank wet?"

"Those are crawfish boring through," I said.

"Phwat's them, sor?"

I explained to him that the crawfish burrowed into the levee from the riverside and that the water naturally followed them, and that by and by they got through on the land side, and that if thousands of them were working through near together the walls between them would crumble and make a great hole through which the river would pour in a crevasse, ruining vast stretches of land and the crops and the people.

"Howly Mother, and do they do that?" he asked.

I told him that people had to be on the watch for their mischief all the time.

"I'd like to see one of them," said Tim, and when we found one he cried out:

"Bedad, it's a lobsther that's young, and phawt a dale he has to grow; but, sor, ain't it so that now he's little he ates up the paple, and phwen he's grown the paple ates up him. But, sor, the mischief he does for one so schmall!" Then turning soberly to me, he said:

"Begob, the divil's that little, I dunno; and it's little divils that does the worst for us byes."

We were marching in brigade column one day, with all the baggage trains, the artillery, the pontoons, and the camp-followers, when we came across an old negro who was leaning upon his frail wicket-gate in front of his cabin, gazing in amazement on the passing men. I rode up to him and said:

"Well, uncle, this is a good many men who are marching by, isn't it?"

"Laws, marse," said he, "I never dreampt dere was so many men in the worl' befo'."

"And well ye may say it," said Tim, "and that's phwat the whole southern confederacy will be thinkin' afore we're done wid 'em."

TIM HICKEY AND THE FLAG.

There came to the beach a poor exile of Erin,
The dew on his thin robe was heavy and chill;
For his country he sighed, when at twilight repairing,
To wander alone by the wind-beaten hill.—Campbell.

The tear that we shed, though in secret it rolls,
Shall long keep his memory green in our souls.—Moore.

UR ARMY was made up of all sorts and pretty much all nationalities of men; but where we had been with what we call foreigners —though most of us have but to look back a few generations to find we are such too—we lost the idea that they were aliens, and our commingled blood helped to cement the bond that was formed by our suffering together in march and bivouac and camp, in hunger, thirst and fatigue, and sometimes in sickness and comrade-care. So we forgot that Tim was an Irishman, and even his speech with its rollicking brogue wasn't more different from ours than was the "daown-east" Yankee's from that of the New Yorker, or either of them from the mountain Tennesseean.

But Tim showed us how that sense of nationality was lost, at the last.

In one of our great battles the order came for a charge all along the line. Our regiment was to make

"Coom on, byes."

it across a last year's cotton-field, and on the enemy whose glistening bayonets we could see in a chapperell on the other side. It looked like grim death.

When the order came Tim sprang out before the line, and swinging his hat, cried:

"Coom on, byes! Coom on! We're goin' to the slaughter-house! Don't ye feel the rope a-danglin' round yer hor-r-ns?"

The yell that came in answer from the men, maybe, did as much as anything to give us the day, for that charge broke the enemy, and we were soon chasing them. Then all that remained was to shell the woods, while broken companies rallied to see what was left.

The hurried roll-call came, and Tim Hickey's name was called.

"Tim Hickey!" No response.

"Tim Hickey!" louder. Still no response.

"Boys, never mind the roll; let's find Tim!"

Over that cotton-field they ranged, turning over a body that was face down to see if it might be Tim, and wiping off the clotted blood and brains and mud; giving a poor fellow who was wounded a sup of water out of canteen—searching for Tim. All at once a voice came from off to the right of our line, from a fellow lying propped on his elbow and with his head on his hand:

"Byes, maybe it's Tim ye're afther. Here's phwats left o' him."

They got him gently from the field, and all were tender with our loved Tim, though the surgeon shook his head as he examined his wounds. In the hospital the boys would get up to him when they could with a cup of wild strawberries or a bunch of wild-wood flowers that they had braved the wood-ticks to pick.

They got him gently from the field.

One day, when I went up to see him, they had moved his cot so that the head of it was by a window in the court-house that had been made into a hospital and that stood in the middle of the plaza. Tim was looking over the top of his head and into the sky, out of the window.

"What is it, Tim?" I asked.

"D'ye moind, sorr," said he. "It's the ould flag at the head of the flag-schtaff. I was thinkin,' sorr, it was loike an angel up there, and was a floatin' loike, watching Tim. For, sorr, I done me besht, God knows. But, sorr, I'm gettin' waker—I know it well—and I'm thinkin,' sorr, I mayn't hit another lick for the ould flag. Oh, sorr, if yez live to git home, sorr, ye know where I live, not far out o' La Porte, sorr; wud it be too much for ye to foind me Biddy and tell her Tim died loike the man she tuck him to be?"

Tim seemed faint and the pallor deepened in his face, but his eyes gleamed. I gave him some water, and rousing up, he said:

"It gits me now and then, the hurt, sorr, that lets me feel faint-loike afther; but I want to tell yez, sorr. We had a bit cabin in the ould counthry, and a cow, and a pig or two, and they was disthrained for rint, sorr. I came to America, and left Biddy and the childher there; and I found work on a railroad wid a shovel and a pick; and I didn't dhrink a dhrop, sorr; I didn't even schmoke—I, saving the money for Biddy to come. By and by I got 'em here, sorr, and we both worked; me a diggin' and Biddy a washin' and clanin'; and we saved up till we've got our home,

TIM HICKEY AND THE FLAG.

sorr, and it's moine; and a cow, and she's moine; and a pig or two, and they're moine; and all's paid for, and divil a disthraint can come.

"Tell Biddy"—here came a gasp and a contraction of pain, and I wet his lips with water—"tell Biddy that, dear as the ould green flag wid the harp in it of Ireland is, that—this is our—flag, and this—is our counthry—and, sorr, tell—her to tache—the childer—to love the—flag that—their father loved—and—Howly Mother of God, the—flag—is a—bright—angel—he's—come!"

Tim was dead.

RAW OFFICERS.

Ay me! what perils do environ
The man that meddles with cold iron!
What plaguy mischiefs and mishaps
Do dog him still with after-claps!—Hudibras.

He stands erect; his slouch becomes a walk,
He steps right onward, martial in his air,
His form and movement.—Cowper.

AS WE look back upon the war and realize how illy we were prepared for our great responsibilities in the taking of commands, through our lack of a military education, many of those who became officers coming from the life of civilians and never having had the drill of even the National Guards of the different states from which they came, and by whose Governors they were commissioned, it is remarkable, not only how well the men were maneuvered, but that the success of our arms was what it was. Yet we worked for it, studying our school for the soldier, and for the company, and for the battalion. Gen. Garfield used to work over formations by the aid of blocks of wood that represented squads, and then companies, and then regiments.

There were in the ranks men of all trades.

But the men who became officers were intelligent and educated. Even our private soldiers were, many of them, scholarly men, not a few graduates from our colleges, and whole companies were made up of undergraduates. There were in the ranks men of all trades, and many from the learned professions, so that nothing was needed to be done, from the building of a bridge to the manning of a hospital, but experts sprang to the call for volunteers to carry the matter through.

But in military affairs the beginnings of those who might afterward become celebrated in their commands were pitiable enough, even of men who came out of the service with stars in their shoulder-straps and their coat buttons arranged in twos and threes. We have to remember that the first commission of most of our volunteer company officers was through the suffrages of the men who had been enlisted by them, and who often were fellow-townsmen.

While I was commanding a military district, which meant a recruiting station and a camp of instruction, a raw, red-headed man came into headquarters and announced that he had brought a company of a hundred men for muster-in. I told him to go out and get them in line and I would look them over. When I went to the parade ground he stood before a rabble of men and was scratching his tawny head, trying to think of the necessary order, and at last he shouted, with some interlarded profanity:

"Get into rows! Get into rows! Ain't they any military about ye?"

Yet that man became one of the best drill-masters in his regiment, and his company was one of the best in the command, both in discipline and tactics.

A captain who afterwards became a distinguished major-general forgot the form when he wanted to march his company by the flank, and gave the order:

"Go endways!"

"Get into rows! Get into rows! Ain't there any military about ye?"

When he wanted to march them through the gap in a fence his order was:

"Break ranks, and form on the other side."*

A celebrated officer, who afterward became Governor of his state, tells me that when he was tendered a command, he went to a regular army officer with whom he was intimate and said to him:

"Now, don't give me away, but just tell me, which is the ranking officer in a regiment, a major or an adjutant or a colonel?"

And then he asked, still under the ban of secrecy:

"Does a major go afoot, or ride horseback?"

I have heard of a New England captain who, in wishing to march his company to the right, ordered them to "Gee." More surprising things have occurred, and it does not at all follow that that officer did not become the perfection of a drill-master, and a very martinet in discipline.

Perhaps the hardest thing an officer had to overcome

---

*I see that in the "Life of Abraham Lincoln," edited by Ida M. Tarbell (McClure's Magazine, January, 1896, p. 130), this unique military order is credited to the "Great Emancipator," and in his own words: "I could not for the life of me," said he, "remember the proper word of command for getting my company endways, so that it could get through the gate; so as we came near the gate I shouted, 'This company is dismissed for two minutes, when it will fall in again on the other side of the gate.'" This may be so. I remember that Henry Ward Beecher once said that a striking remark once credited to him had been before referred to his father, and probably to some prominent man in every generation since Calvin. Maybe Napoleon and Alexander, each in turn, had ordered a company to "go endways"; but the story was current during the war as above.

RAW OFFICERS.

was the sense of equality on the part of his men, who, as townsmen, had always been in the habit of calling him Bill or Tom at home, and who felt that he was putting on unwarranted airs in assuming the station of command, and a position upon which they could not intrude.

But it was one of the remarkable things of our volunteer system, and was a rare tribute to the good sense of our citizen soldiery, that they very quickly recognized the necessity for this, and adapted themselves to it.

THE DEVOTED MAJOR.

Man is of soul and body, formed for deeds of high resolve,
on fancy's boldest wing.—Shelley.

Greater love hath no man than this, that a man lay down
his life for his friends.—John, 15:13.

OR second major of his regiment the colonel of —— regiment of —— cavalry had a cynical man who, though admirable in drill and discipline, was, to say the least, self-contained, holding little in common with the other officers or with his commander. He was punctilious in all points of official courtesy and of military etiquette, yet the colonel had an idea that he disliked him, though why he had no conception. Morose, sad of countenance, never seen to smile, he stood by himself, and seemed to desire to do so. Yet he was brave to a fault and never seemed so happy as when on some dangerous duty, and especially if it had in it a bit of dash with a hot cross-country pursuit of a band of guerillas.

One day while marching the major rode, silent and

THE DEVOTED MAJOR. 37

evidently buried in his own thoughts, just at the colonel's left at the head of the column, when a fire was opened on the videttes, that showed an ambuscade. Ordering after him the company that was on the right

"Thank God, I took that bullet for you, sir."

of column, the colonel dashed on to the support of his advance, and soon was in the thick of a hand-to-hand fight with sabres and pistols. All at once the major dashed his horse up by the side of the colonel's, almost dismounting that officer, and, as he turned angrily to rebuke him, he saw that the major was wounded, and caught him just in time to prevent his falling from his horse. In a husky voice the major said:

"Thank God, I took that bullet for you, sir!"

The fight was soon over and the wounded major was taken to his tent, while the surgeon, after examination, said that the ball, seeming to have touched no vital spot, appeared to be lodged in the spine and he was afraid it meant the paralysis of the body below the thigh. It seems the major had seen a carbine aimed at the colonel, and, too late to strike it up, he had plunged in to make of himself a barrier to it. Then it was revealed that under all his taciturnity and apparent acerbity of disposition, there was a deep affection, and especially for his colonel, that made any self-sacrifice possible.

With this most unexpected display of devotion his whole nature seemed to change, and he hung upon the visits that his commander made often in the day. Though he gave no inkling of any cause of sadness in his life, it was evident that some dark cloud hung over it; but the colonel's coming seemed to be a gleam of sunshine shot into his tent, and was always greeted with a smile and a cordial hand-shake, while hearty laughs—the first anyone had ever heard—gave token of his enjoyment of the colonel's sallies of wit, for he carried no sad and long-drawn face to his wounded major, who had exemplified the words of that other Savior, "Greater love hath no man than this, that a man lay down his life for his friend."

The colonel had a very beautiful watch of rare and singular workmanship, and the major, with the simplicity that often comes to a wounded man, loved to hold it and examine it as he lay on his cot. One day the colonel said:

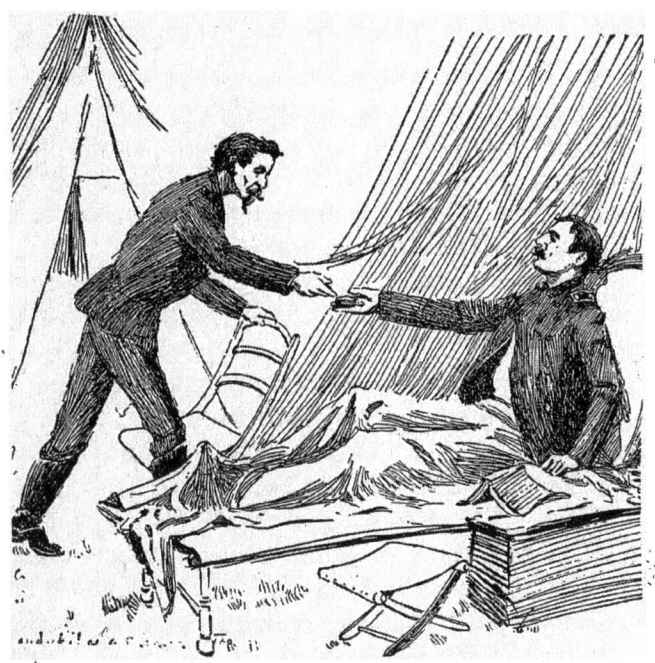

"Take mine, and let it be a memento, too."

"Major, you have done the greatest thing for me that ever a man could do for another, and anything I have that you fancy I will gladly give you. Just keep that watch, if you fancy it, and let it be a memento of what you have done for your only too grateful colonel. Send it down to your oldest son."

Tears welled up into the major's eyes, and taking up his own watch, which was a plain gold one, he handed it to the colonel, saying:

"Well, I don't need two watches. I accept yours, and it shall go to my oldest boy when he comes to be of age. Take mine, and let it be a memento, too, and to go in the same way."

The major was taken home after a while, and when the regiment went back to its state for muster-out, he was brought to the capital to see "the boys" once more. His greeting to his colonel was even effusive; but one day the colonel said:

"Major, I gave you my watch in the South one day, and I see you have it with you. I wish you would give it back to me."

In a burst of rage the major handed it to him and turned away his rolling chair from him. Two days passed and the colonel called again on his friend, who received him most icily, and said:

"Old fellow, it was a mean test of your confidence in your old colonel, and it don't seem to have worked. But here is your watch again."

"I don't want your —— watch!"

"Open it and see, major."

The major did so and saw inscribed within a history of his heroism and self-sacrifice.

"I knew," said the colonel, "that you would never half tell your boy the story of your grand work, and now he'll know it from me; so will generations of your blessed family as the watch goes from one to another."

The major was overcome, and just put his hand into that of the colonel as he said:

"I haven't a word to say!"

THE SHARP-SHOOTERS.

A fool's bolt is soon shot.—Henry V., Act III., Scene 7.

To be the aim of every dangerous shot.—Richard III., Act IV., Scene 4.

HE COLONEL commanding the brigade gave me the story: He was sitting on his horse, alone in the field, having sent off all his aids with orders to different regiments of his command, and the general commanding the division joined him to give him some orders for the disposition of his troops. The colonel had on a little vizorless fur cap that he fancied. All at once the general said:

"Colonel, the sharpshooters are firing at your fur cap. It is a distinguishing badge. You'd better take it off and throw it away. I haven't heard the bullets 'zipping' so all day as since I have been here."

"Well," said the colonel, "I haven't noticed it till you spoke of it. They do come pretty thick. But if they

"Colonel, the sharpshooters are firing at your fur cap."

are firing so wide of the mark as that I think I'll continue to risk it."

There came a sound "zip-thug-g!" and the general said:

"There! that ball struck you!"

"No, I haven't felt it."

"Then it struck your horse."

"No, I haven't felt him quiver."

"I'm going to see where it hit," said the general as he dismounted. He looked about and found that it had struck a stump over which the colonel's horse was standing.

"There it is," he said. "They've got the range, but are too low. It was a close call for your *sole*."

"Well, if they keep as far from my intangible soul as that they won't bring it to earth."

"Now, then, for business," said the general, and the subject was dismissed.

The colonel was not hit by those sharpshooters, and the general assured him it was because he was by him, as he said neither he nor any of his staff had ever been wounded, and he was sure the bullet was not cast that could touch any one who was with him.

Months afterward we had a great battle in the southwest, which proved to be the last, in that section, of the war, and the colonel's brigade was engaged. The Union arms were victorious and a good many prisoners had been taken. The colonel was a kind-hearted man, and knowing the deprivations of the Confederates, and wishing to lighten the horrors of capture, he was accustomed to have cut up into small chunks a lot of tobacco and carry it round to the poor fellows—having a darky or two take it in buckets—as the greatest solace they could have.

The command that had been opposed to him in Tennessee, at the time I have spoken of, had been in this battle also, and as he still wore the same little fur cap, he was recognized by one of the prisoners, who said:

"Half a dozen of us fellows, all crack shots, were firing at you."

"Weren't you commanding a brigade at the battle of ——?"

"Yes," said the colonel.

"Well, half a dozen of us fellows, all crack shots, were firing at you for an hour. We thought you had a charmed life, and one of the fellows pounded together a silver piece to see if that wouldn't fetch you. We got scared after a while 'coz we couldn't hit you, for we were the picked sharpshooters of the regiment, and any one of us could have split a ball on a knife stuck in a tree."

And then, as the colonel told me the story, he laughed, and said that the fellow got mad at him because he told him that his safety probably lay in the fact that they had aimed at him all the time.

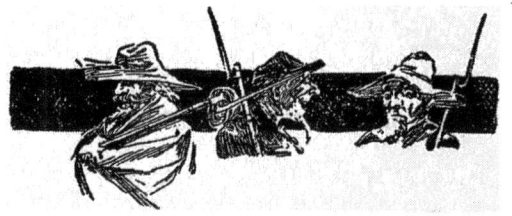

BOYS.

And after all what is a lie? 'Tis but
The truth in masquerade.—Byron.

The foreground of human life is the only part of it which we can examine with real exactness.—Froude.

"OYS" was a common name for our soldiers. It was not so far wrong when we realize that the average age of the army of the Potomac was given me from Washington as twenty-two years. I mentioned that fact once at the reunion of the regiment of which the celebrated Rev. Henry Clay Trumbull was chaplain, and he said his regiment would better that, for that their average age was only eighteen. Young boys would try by every means to get into the service, offering themselves as drummer-boys, or for any position, so they might be accepted and mustered in.

A little fellow came to me one day and said he wanted to enlist. I told him he was too young, but he

.insisted that he was older than he looked and was old enough.

"Are you over eighteen?" I asked.

"Yes, sir," he answered in perfect frankness.

I told him he must wait till the mustering officer

Young boys would try every means to get into the service.

came and we would see. As that officer went down the line looking over the men he stopped before this bright little fellow and said:

"What's this we've got? Are we robbing cradles?

Here, chick, you'd better go home to your mother."

I told him that the boy said he was over eighteen, and if he was I didn't want to lose him, for he looked like a plucky little fellow and would have the making of a good cavalryman, even if I had to detail him as orderly at headquarters.

"Are you over eighteen, my boy?" asked the officer.

"Yes, sir," said the boy.

"Are you ready to swear that you are over eighteen?"

"Yes, sir."

"Do you know the nature of an oath?"

"Yes, sir."

"Well, what is it?"

"If I tell a lie I'll never have no hope for heaven, and I'll be damned to all eternity."

"Well, you do know what an oath means. Now, with that awful penalty are you prepared to swear that you are over eighteen?"

"Yes, sir."

"I don't see," said the mustering officer to me, "what is left but for me to take the kid, though I believe in my heart he's lying."

I told him to go ahead and muster him in, for I wanted the boy. So he gave him the oath.

After the muster was over, and the mustering officer had gone, I sent for the little soldier, and when he came into my tent I said to him:

"I'm afraid you lied and perjured yourself. Now, my boy, you are mustered into the service and you can't get out, and no one can take you out. Look

Taking off his shoe he showed me a card.

into my eye and tell me, are you over eighteen years old?"

"Oh, no, sir," said he.

"Why," I said, greatly startled, "didn't you swear that you were?"

"No, sir," said he. "You didn't either of you ask me if I was over eighteen *years old*, you only asked if I was over eighteen, and I was, and I am," and taking off his shoe he showed me a card on which was the figure "18," and he had been standing on it.

Before the war was over that little fellow was over eighteen years old, and he had chevrons on his sleeve. I had him for orderly for a time, but he was too valuable a man for such a position, and went back to his company to step into the line of promotion.

THE BUGLER.

The silver snarling trumpets 'gan to chide.—Keats.

The thing became a trumpet, whence he blew
Soul animating strains.   —Wordsworth.

Hark! the shrill trumpet sounds to horse! away!
My soul's in arms, and eager for the fray.—Colley Cibber.

COLONEL NAGELEY had his regiment about full, up to the complement of twelve hundred and forty-seven men, counting both field and line; and was doing the best he could at his Camp of Instruction to get men and horses in shape at company and battalion drill; but he was not satisfied with the progress of his buglers—not even the man who was acting as chief-bugler. They were bunglers instead—so much difference one letter put into a word will make. The Camp of Instruction was in the Colonel's home town, and where he felt he knew everybody.

One day a fine-looking young man stood before his tent-opening, and touched his cap as the Colonel looked up from his camp-desk to see who shut off his sunlight.

"Well, my young friend, what is it?" asked the Colonel, somewhat brusquely.

"I want to go into the army," said the young man.

"What is your name?"

"Guido Caracci."

"Italian?"

"My father's parents were from Italy, but I was born in this country, and have never been out of it."

"Caracci? Isn't your father the leader of the town band?"

"Yes, sir."

"Are you a musician, too?"

"I taught the Academy band, sir, that you were so kind as to compliment last Fourth of July. Your praise of it paid me for all the work I put on it."

"Are you able to play any brass instrument?"

"A person who teaches a band rather needs to be able to do something with every instrument, that he may show fellows where they fail."

"Can you play anything else?"

"I'm organist at the Catholic church here in town."

"Well, can you give the calls on a bugle?"

"I've been working at them to commit them to memory for these two months," said the young man with an air of satisfaction.

"H'm! Can you ride horseback?" asked the Colonel.

"You were at our Polo game last week. I heard what you said about my handling my pony."

"What! was it you who rode that little piebald?"

"Yes, sir."

"Can you be here at three o'clock this afternoon, with your horse?"

"Certainly, I can; and with pleasure, if there's anything I can do."

"Do you own a bugle?"

The young man took out from under his coat a small, battered brass bugle that looked as if it might have seen service in the Revolutionary war, and said, "I have only this."

"Sound me the reveille," said the Colonel.

The boy put his bugle to his lips and, clear and sweet, sounded forth the thrill of that exquisite melody, with never a false or faltering note.

"Ah!" thought the Colonel—

> "'One blast upon his bugle horn
> Were worth a thousand men;'"

but he only said:

"How old are you, Guido?"

"Nineteen last September, sir."

"You will be here promptly at three?"

"Yes, sir,"—and the boy was gone.

The Colonel rode to town, found the elder Caracci, and learned that the father had no objection to his son's enlisting; and was told by quite a number of the excellent character of the boy; returned to his tent happy in the thought that not only might he have a good bugler, but one who could teach the others and, perhaps, work up a regimental band — at least of bugles.

THE BUGLER. 55

Precisely at three o'clock the Colonel went afield to take command of his regiment in battalion drill; and Guido, on his piebald pony and with his poor little bugle at his side, rode with him. Order after order was given in quick succession, and was as quickly interpreted by the bugle, clear-cut and faultless, and with never a mistake in a call. The Colonel was charmed.

The upshot was that Guido became a bugler in the regiment; and, just before the command went to the front, the Colonel called him into the tent, and said:

"You have faithfully discharged your duties so far, and I hear you practicing with all the buglers for a band in two parts. I am very much pleased that you have the good will of the company buglers; and now, as a spur to your good work, I want you to take possession of the box that is behind the mess-chest. You can examine it, and see if it will please you."

Guido sprang to get the box, and opening it found a beautiful silver bugle, gold lined; and on it was engraved:

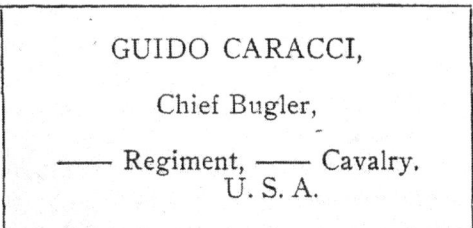

GUIDO CARACCI,

Chief Bugler,

—— Regiment, —— Cavalry.
U. S. A.

Tears started in his eyes, and his voice trembled as he said in amazement, and as if to himself:

"Chief-bugler!"

"It will be announced at dress-parade this evening, if you would like to take the position."

All the happy Guido could say was, "Oh, my God!"

"Try the bugle, and see if it is well toned," said the Colonel.

Choking down a lump in his throat, the boy put to his lips the bright source of his joy, and made the air ring with the music that is dear to both trooper and horse; till the men gathered round to listen, and the picketed horses pricked up their ears and nickered their recognition.

When dress parade was formed and the time came for the band, in place of the silence that had always seemed to the Colonel such a hiatus (except when he had hired the town band), at the order of the Adjutant, and as a surprise to the Commander, the whole corps of buglers, who had been gathered at the right of the line, led by Guido with his new silver bugle, marched down the line playing in two parts a pathetic little melody that Guido had written for them; and returning they played in quicker time a soul-stirring duet, that only the discipline of the command kept the men from applauding.

At "orders" the appointment was announced of Guido Caracci as chief-bugler of the regiment. It was a happy day for the lad, who was welcomed, after the parade was dismissed, with shouts of joy by both buglers and men. The "playing-off" of the bugle band had been a success, as it was also a surprise to both officers and men. But the Adjutant had been in the secret.

Guido remained with the regiment until the Colonel was assigned a brigade of cavalry, and was then detailed as his bugler—since no one could take his place in the Colonel's estimation. He had trained a full band for the regiment, and it was often called to brigade headquarters, where there was a let-up to active service and an evening could be given to music, for it had been under a faithful drill-master.

JINGLE.

His patient soul endures what Heaven ordains,
But neither feels nor fears ideal pains.—Crabbe.

It is a truth but too well known, that rashness attends youth.—Cicero.

FRIEND of mine who was afraid that his son of some sixteen years old would run away and enlist, as so many boys did in their abounding patriotism, arranged for him to go with me, the father bearing all expenses, with the understanding that while he took all the hardships of the service he was not to be unnecessarily exposed to its dangers; and, anyhow, was not to go into battle. He was a bright, plucky little fellow, and gladly took service as the men did. Somewhere he came into possession of a pair of enormous Mexican spurs, with their two-inch steel rowels and the danglers, and with broad leathers which covered the whole upper part of his shoe. As he had no horse and always walked, and as he invariably wore his spurs, his approach was heralded by the jingle of his great adornments—and hence the name by which he came to be universally known, till, I think, most of the men forgot his real name.

When our command was to take a march over the Ozark Mountains, and in order that the men might

For all he knew, he might have been shooting at our own men.

be reduced to the lightest marching order, new clothes and shoes were issued to them, and Jingle got them with the rest. A few days out there came on rain and snow combined, and the shoes of the men began to fall to pieces, as they were soaked with the wet. They were made of paper. Then the pantaloons began to slough off at the bottoms. They were made of a species of felt that was shoddy indeed. Ah, the men *felt* it all, for they were marching bare-footed and bare-legged through the mud and melting snow; except that the spurs kept the heels of Jingle's shoes on. I passed the little fellow on the march, and lifting up his bare and mud-cased leg he gave it a slap and cheerily cried: "Don't I love my country!"

In one of our heavy battles Jingle was left back at headquarters with orders to stay there; but while the battle was at its hottest word came to me that he had been killed. I didn't know how it could be, but thought if he was dead, it was only one more of all the gallant fellows who were falling on every side. But, by and by, word came that he was not dead, but that his leg was badly broken and he was lying by the tent in great agony. As soon as I could I got a surgeon to set the broken limb, and Jingle was made as comfortable as possible.

It seems that, determined to see the fight, he had caught a horse from which some poor fellow had been shot, and getting hold of a Sharp's rifle that was charged in all its chambers, he had made the best use of his heavy-roweled spurs and had got between the lines, where he sat and fired on the enemy (though, for all he knew, he might have been shooting at our own men). As he described it, a detachment of rebel cavalry rode out, knocked his horse down and crushed his leg under it, and rode back, laughing.

Jingle wasn't the only one of us hurt at headquarters, and one day as he lay, groaning and sometimes doing more than to groan, for he had a pretty free English tongue, I said to him:

"Jingle, if you are to be a soldier, you must bear pain better than that. Put your teeth together and 'grin and bear it' like a man. You aren't the only one that has to bear pain."

"Did you suppose it was the pain that made me

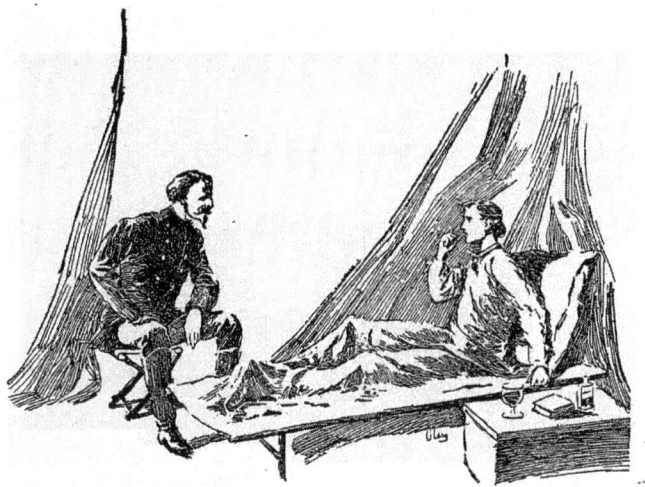

"The idea that it should be done by a horse."

grunt?" snapped out the plucky little fellow. "The idea that it should be done by a horse!"

We had a surgeon in our command with one of those pure, clean, sweet faces that leads one to reverence as well as love it; a man whose life backed up his face, and whose coming into the hospital was always a benediction. One day, as he was dressing Jingle's leg, and the poor boy, though he had shut together his teeth, could not prevent some tears from squeezing between his eyelids, he put his hand on the plucky little fellow's head and said:

"Jingle, when it hurts so badly that you think you can't stand it, anyhow, just remember that our Lord Jesus Christ was hurt ever so much more than you are, and he couldn't even lie down!"

"LITTLE WES."

First gate: "Be bold!" Second gate: "Be bold, be bold, and evermore be bold." Third gate: "Be not too bold."—
Gates of Bosyrane.

> It was great pity, so it was,
> That villainous saltpetre should be digged
> Out of the bowels of the harmless earth,
> Which many a good tall fellow had destroyed
> So cowardly; and but for these vile guns
> He would himself have been a soldier.
> —Henry IV., Part I., Scene 3.

I HAD two darkies at headquarters, both of whom were named Wesley, and were called "Wes" for short. One was over six feet high and the other was much smaller, so they were distinguished as "Big Wes" and "Little Wes." Of the former I shall tell elsewhere. "Little Wes" was an unconscionable darky who would bear watching.

One evening an orderly said to me:

"If you'll take a squad of men and go outside the lines a bit I think I can show you something that will interest you and that you ought to see."

So, making a detail, we rode for a couple of miles or so, and came upon a negro log cabin with the mud knocked from the chinks between the logs, and there, inside and leading a cake-walk dance of the colored people, was Wes in my best uniform—the whole of it, to chapeau, sash, patent-leather boots and spurs. The reek of the room reached us on the outside. As I led him out by the ear and demanded what he meant by spoiling a suit of clothes that had cost me a hundred and fifty dollars, he gave a negro chuckle, showing all his gleaming teeth, and said:

"Lord, marse, I'se dun had 'em!"

That was Little Wes.

In one of our battles I was trying to take a raw regiment that had never been under a heavy fire across in the rear of a battery to form them on the right and rear. Old soldiers will recognize the fact that a regiment was never placed directly in the rear of an active battery.

As we got into the range of the guns an orderly rode by me and the head of the column, and whether the horse was running away with him or he was himself frightened and did not know he had passed us I never knew. A six-pound round shot went through the horse just back of the orderly's knees, and he came down, while his rider, landing on his feet, made for the rear with no word to me. I had to march the boys by that disemboweled, dying horse, and soon after a shell exploded over the center of the column, striking down some men. It was of no use. I ordered the men on their faces, and they hugged the ground so

Leading a cake-walk dance, was Wes in my best uniform.

close that they seemed to dent it. While I was standing at the right of my prostrate line, rather seeing to it that there were a number of trees between me and the battery, Little Wes came dancing down to me and said:

We never could get Little Wes near enough to a fight to smell powder again.

"Marse Colonel, may I go down dere and see dem big guns shoot?"

"It's pretty hot over there, Wes," I said.

"Laws, marse, I'se brung up in de Souf, and I can stan' de heat as well's any cullud boy."

I thought if this darky was so brave and cool I

LITTLE WES.

could shame my boys to their feet at sight of it, and so I told Wes he could go.

He sat on a bend of the snake fence three or four panels from our battery, and when a shell would go overhead with its "whur-ra-whur-ra" he'd follow its course with his upturned face, and then he'd shout. When our guns went off he'd throw up his hat and give a darky whoop. I was just telling our boys to see that a nigger could be braver than a white man, and was ordering them to their feet, when a round shot struck the panel of the fence next the one Wes was on, knocking it into splinters and sending him and his bend of the fence to the ground. He came running back to me with eyes distended, cheeks ashy and his hair seeming to come out of kink, as he shouted:

"Ma-marse C-c-colonel, d-did you s-s-see dat dar? Deys d-d-done sh-shootin' iron bullets d-d-down dar! I'se gwine t' d' rear!"

We never could get Little Wes near enough to a fight to smell powder again.

"BIG WES."

They (the blacks) had no rights which the white man was bound to respect.—Judge Taney, Dred Scott case.
"Homo homini aut deus aub lupus."
[Man is to man either a god or a wolf.]—Erasmus.

Whatever day
Makes man a slave, takes half his worth away.—Pope.

ARCHING up through Mississippi, in the latter part of the war, I saw off to the right and beyond our flankers a squad of people evidently making for the woods; and, as we never allowed anything of the kind to go without knowing all about it, I called for a couple of platoons of men from the head of the column and dashed off to investigate. I found it was a man with a lot of negroes manacled together with handcuffs, and evidently endeavoring to get out of our way. I asked the man what he was doing with these people, and he told me he was taking them down to Texas, where the Emancipation Proclamation was not in

"CYAN'T I GO WID YOU ON DE BOAT TO YO' HOME?"

force, as, for that matter, it was not in Louisiana. I told him that these slaves were all free, and ordered him to unlock the handcuffs. He told me to go to a place from which every good minister is trying to warn his people. So I ordered one of my men to knock him down, take away his keys and set them free. This he did, with a good heart. Then I told the colored people that they could join our negro-help and come with us; and the man I had tied to the tail of a mule and brought him along.

There must have been an affinity between that man and the mule, for it was the only day in which that animal's heels had not been in the air for a good share of the time. He did not kick once all day. I am sure he was more humane than I, or he had not had his heart so touched at sight of the inhuman cruelty to the poor negroes.

Among the colored people so set free was an enormous negro, over six feet tall, and with large limbs and every showing of herculean strength, and he had been manacled to a woman, whose smaller wrist was held by the steel handcuff, which had almost buried itself in the flesh of her gigantic companion in misery. He told me that his name was "Wesley." So, with the smaller Wesley about headquarters, he came to be known as "Big Wes." I told him he might join the headquarter-servants, do the work about the stables and tent that fell to his lot, and draw rations with the others.

For days he was about my quarters, black, surly,

70 CAMP FIRE STORIES.

ugly in every look and evidently with hatred in his heart. One day I said to him:

"Why can't you put on a pleasant face and not be looking always like a thunder-cloud? You depress

"It's me. It's Wes come back."

me. Don't you get enough to eat and have plenty of sleep and light enough work?"

"Yas, marse," said he in the same grum tone. "I'se nothin' but a nigger and a slave. T'oder day I b'long to dat man, now I b'long to you. I ain't no free man."

"I can't prevent your being a negro," I said, "but you are free—free as air. You are more free than I am, for I must get permission from Washington if I want to go anywhere. You can drown yourself in the Mississippi if you want to for all me. I tell you you are perfectly free."

"Does you mean to tell me 'at ef I run away you wouldn't fotch me back?"

"Try it and see," said I. "I tell you you are nothing to me. You can go where you like!"

That night he was gone. Days went by and I had forgotten all about him, when, as I was writing in my tent I became aware of something shutting off my light from the open flaps, and looking up I saw a tall, gaunt specimen done up in ebony, though ashy from hunger and weakness.

"Hello!" I cried. "What's this? A spook?"

"It's me. It's Wes come back. Marse, didn't yo' send for me when I don' runned away?"

"Bless me," I said, "if I had you'd been back within an hour. No, I tell you you are free! But go to the cook and fill up!"

Instead of doing so he fell on his knees and then fairly rolled on the floor, crying, laughing, praying, shouting, and wanted even to embrace my feet.

"Oh, de bressed Lo'd Jesus! I'se free! I'se free! Oh, the holy chariot! I'se don' free; I is, I is!"

Well, I sent him finally to make up for his long fast; for he had eaten nothing but nuts and roots in his

72   CAMP FIRE STORIES.

hiding. But he was transformed into one of the happiest, jolliest and most useful men about the corral, and certainly his devotion to me was akin to worship.

When the time came for the regiment to go home for the muster-out, I told Big Wes that we were to re-

Big Wes was a delight to the children.

turn North, and that he'd better get him some girl for a wife and make a home down there among his people and in the warm South.

"Cyan't I go wid you on de boat to yo' home?" he asked.

"No," I said; "what could you do there? I need no

servant, and you'd freeze to death in one of our winters."

"Well, marse," said he, while his ample lips took on a hard, firm look, "I'se don' got from de major dat lives in yo' town de name on a piece of paper and de showin' of de way, and I'll be dar in time."

"What do you mean, Wes? Are you going to try and walk up there?"

"Yes, marse. I cyan't never live away from the man 'at sot me free."

Well, with such devotion as that I couldn't refuse, and so took him with us on the boat. He was in my family thence on, till I decided to go to Minnesota, doing my odd chores about the house and stable, a delight to the children and to the little mother, and working at odd jobs about town for the balance of the time. He could do the work of two men in a day, and brought me his earnings, which I put into the safe.

I told him that Minnesota was almost too cold for a white man, and he'd better take his earnings and buy him a little farm somewhere near by, and the major would help him about his payments. So he did, and the last I heard of him he had married and raised a family, had been steadily to night-school till he had learned to read and write and cipher, and now is a man who is rich for his station in life.

DISCOMFORTS.

But man is a carnivorous production
  And must have meals, at least one meal a day;
He cannot live, like woodcocks, upon suction,
  But, like the shark and tiger, must have prey.
                            —Byron.

"Me pinguem et nitidum bene curata cute vises,
  *   *   * Epicuri de grege porcum."
[You may see me, fat and shining with well cared for hide
*   *   * a hog from Epicurus' herd.]—Horace.

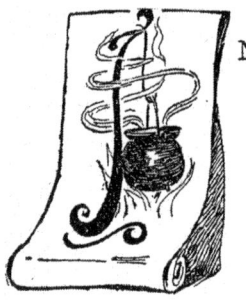

N SOUTHWEST Missouri, during the early part of the war, we were far away from the base of supplies and had, as we suspected, the commissary stores that were left over from the Mexican war. Our hard-tack was hard indeed. It was said to have been made by a Benjamin Cozzens, but we all knew that the "B. C." stamped on it meant that it was made Before Christ. If we laid a bit of bacon on a fence rail to take a sup of coffee we had to hold it to keep it there. It reminded me of a story of Charles Lamb, who, having some guests come late one evening, was asked by his

DISCOMFORTS. 75

sister Mary to go to the grocer's for some supplies. The grocer was weighing out some cheese, and said:

"Mr. Lamb, my store-boy is gone home, may I do this up in a paper and let you carry it with you?"

"N-no," said Mr. Lamb, "if you'll t-t-tie a st-st-string round it I'll l-l-lead it home!"

A law had been announced that we were to kill no domestic animals—meaning the hogs that roamed the woods and which were called "razor-backs," and of whom the soldiers said if you wanted to see if they were fat enough to kill, you took them up by the ears to see if the nose would balance the tail; and we were forbidden to burn the fences—though that was afterwards modified and we were permitted to take the top rail, which was all we ever wanted to take.

Sometimes that order was pretty hard on the boys, as in the case of one night, after a hard march in the rain all day, and when our camp was a wet bivouac; for, though we did have "spring-beds," they were not comfortable since the spring came out of the foot-hills.

There were several stacks of threshed-out straw near by, and adjoining some large barns and a mill, and these were levied on by the wet and chilled soldiers for beds. But complaint was made by the disloyal old farmer and he gloated over the "northern mud-sills," as they were obliged to carry back all the straw.

The next morning when we were on our march a lurid light far at the rear showed that the stacks had been fired. The general commanding rode up to an officer, who sympathized with the suffering men, and

He gloated over the "northern mudsills" as they were obliged to carry back all the straw.

ordered him to take a squad and arrest every one who was engaged in that work of revenge. The captain made a detail for the purpose, and sent a man, at the full speed of his horse, to order every man who was near the stacks to stand still till he came to arrest him. When he got there there was not a man to be seen. All had run away. But stacks and barns and mill were all destroyed. The selfish old man had kept the troops in discomfort, as he wished to do, and had gotten back his straw only to help swell the fire.

At one time one of the generals, who was very popular with the men, came to the headquarters of a colonel of cavalry and said:

"Have you got anything to eat? I'm ravenous. You cavalrymen always have something good."

The colonel told him if he would come back in a couple of hours he would have a good dinner for him, to be eaten on the headquarters' mess-chest.

The colonel had an old Frenchman whose name was Ogden for his cook. He had been a cook in Paris, but, coming to this country, had enlisted, and was too old for service; so he had been detailed for the headquarters' kitchen as *chef*. The colonel gave him a revolver and ordered him to get a dinner and have it ready in a couple of hours for Gen. ——.

Ogden had found somewhere, and "pressed," a Yankee-baker. This is a tin affair that is used before a fireplace, and it has in it a spit on which the item to be cooked is impaled, and which is turned by a crank bent in the end of it, outside the Yankee-baker, so that one would imagine that the cook was grinding

He had been a cook in Paris.

a hand-organ, or was winding up a Waterbury watch. But Ogden used the Yankee-baker for a "cover," for he liked to bring in the *piece de resistance* in style.

So, when the general and the colonel were seated at the mess-chest, inhaling the rich fumes of the roast with which the air was filled, Ogden brought in his platter, which was a board, covered by his great tin Yankee-baker.

"Remove the cover," said the colonel; but as Ogden did so the general drew back.

"Oh!" he said, "it is awful. It smells good and I am hungry, but you know the order, Colonel, against killing any domestic animals. How is this?"

"I don't know anything about it, General," said the colonel. "Ask Ogden; he's nobody's fool."

"Ogden," demanded the general, "what about this pig?"

"Zat vat, sare?" asked Ogden.

"Why, this pig!"

"Zat is not a pig, General."

"Why, of course it is. Look at its nose, look at its toes, look at its tail," for Ogden had brought it in cooked whole, as though to leave no doubt about it.

"Oh, general," said Ogden, "a pig is a animile as is put in a sty, and is fed wiz corn and wiz swill, and is made fat and is stick in ze throat and cut up and put in a barrel and make pork!"

"Yes," said the general, "I know that; but what has that to do with this?"

"Well, General, I get on my horse and ride in ze field and through ze woods, and over ze fence, and I just catch up wiz zis animile wiz a bullet. General, a pig cannot run like zat. Zat is not pig; he is possum."

Then, complacently, the general hummed the old tune, "Kyarve dat possum."

I have heard that the soldiers said if they were crossing a field and any man's sheep bit them they'd kill it, and that the sheep were dangerous. So, too, I have heard of a colonel who was calling to account some men who were barbecuing a sheep, threatening guard-house and tying up by the thumbs, but who all at once cried out:

"Turn him, turn him quick. He's burning on the under side!"

I do not know. It may be that these things were so. I've read in the North American Review that if sheep do not bite, yet they are dangerous. I suppose they were in Missouri, for a great many had to be killed by soldiers. Just listen to this:

"A wild sheep in his native country is no trifling antagonist. The horns of the Ovis Poli and Argali are enormous, and must be seen to be appreciated. Sir Joseph Hooker, the great botanist, says that in Thibet foxes have been known to make kennels in the hollow horns of the Argali. This sounds rather a tall statement, and I confess I should much like to find one of these hermit crab-like foxes at home.

"Some Indian tame sheep are desperate fellows to fight, and are exhibited by native potentates matched against bulls and other animals. Phil Robinson tells a story of a ram that was sent to the Calcutta Zoölogical Gardens, and, since he was of no value as a curiosity, the keepers thought that he would make a nice tidbit for a tiger. The sheep, however, being of a pugnacious disposition, "went for" the tiger as soon as he was put in the cage. The traveler goes on to tell that, after a sharp tussle, the sheep killed the tiger. Whether he ate him afterward is not related, but one would not be surprised at anything in such a sheep as that."

AUNT EV.

We may live without poetry, music and art;
We may live without conscience, and live without heart;
We may live without friends; we may live without books;
But civilized man cannot live without cooks.
                                    —Owen Meredith.

Heaven sends us good meat, but the devil sends us cooks.
                                    —Garrick.

                        'Tis burnt; and so is all the meat;
What dogs are these! Where is the rascal cook?
How durst you, villains, bring it from the dresser, and
    serve it thus?—Taming of the Shrew, Act IV, Sc. 1.

UNT EV was an old negress, stooping, wrinkled, grizzled and very likely wicked — of that I don't know — but she was a good cook and adapted to camp as well as to the house.

The way she came to be cook at my Headquarters was this: My command was at the city of ———; in the State of ——— (names of places don't count when I'm speaking of an old woman who has been dead, save in our memories, for these twenty-odd years) and for Headquarters I had a rambling old mansion that had been deserted by its occupants, who had gone further South with the retiring Confederate army when we took possession of the city. Aunt Ev had been left behind because she was too old to be moved. She came into my room as I sat at my desk on the morning that I took possession.

"Marse Kunnel," she said, "I dun want you t' tak' me fer cook yer. I'se cook fer my people sence I was lillie picannin,'—dat is, I'se helper t' d' cook twell I was gal, n' nen cook she die, an' I'se cook for Missy Jul.; an' bimeby I'se took fer d' people. I'se cook fer great house fer forty, sixty year. I knows dis house, kase I'se had d' kitchen allus. Marse, you gimme vittles an' I cook 'em so's you des laugh, dey so good. I do' want pay, on'y home an' 'ere w'ere I'se allus raise; an' ef I gits 'nuff fer pipe an' dippin'-box, an' des lillie whiskey t' git out d' cobwebs fr' m' t'roat in d' mawnin', da's all. I gits m' vittles w'en I gits you'ns. Marse, des dun tak' old Aun' Ev, an' you don' be sorry: you be glad."

So I told her to go down to the kitchen that had always been her home, and directed the Commissary to see that she was supplied with provisions. She drank half a tumbler of "Robinson County" that I poured out for her, and took it raw with never a wink, only exclaiming:

"Oh, Marse Kunnel, I nev' dun tas'e sech befo'. Dat like ile, 'e s' smooth an' sweet. Marse, don' giv' ole nig' sech aller time. Ole Aun' Ev like 'nodder kin', 't cut as 't goes down."

So I assured her that henceforth she might come up before breakfast and the Surgeon would give her real "Commissary," that she'd feel at every gulp till it made her old eyes water. They gleamed at the prospect, until the white circles that old age had faded out of the rims of the irises seemed to have some fire in them.

We had at Headquarters the full field and staff, with quite a corps of orderlies; and I told Aunt Ev to detail some of the colored hangers-on for her helpers in the kitchen and scullery.

My mouth waters now as I look back on the dishes we had at our mess—from "shoat and cabbage" to bacon—both as to the variety and quality of cookery. Maybe our active life, in drills, scouts—almost living on horseback as we did—helped our food to taste good, and fitted us to enjoy what we might not find so toothsome now. But Aunt Ev was a success for all day and every day;—after she had swallowed her morning's dram of a half glass of such whiskey as would have made a white person's hair stand on end.

Things had gone on in this way for a number of weeks to our complete contentment, when I had occasion to go through the kitchen during the process of getting dinner. I had better stayed out; for this is what I saw:

The cooking was carried on in a broad brick fireplace; and on the stone hearth sat Aunt Ev superintending a number of sauce-pans that were upon the coals, while some kettles hung on the pot-hooks of the crane. She was smoking a short, black cob-pipe that was filled with leaf-tobacco as it had come from the curing-house; and her expectorations were aimed at the rear of the fire-place in full faith that they escaped the sauce-pans, and struck under the suspended kettles. By her lay her dipping-box with the "brush" sticking out of it, ready to be resumed when the pipe was exhausted. This, like chewing tobacco (which Aunt Ev did also at odd times), involved more expectoration. I think that, as I took this in, and the evident fact that the same unwashed utensils served for the cooking of dishes that were to follow each other, and the general uncleanliness, led me to exclaim, "Great Scot!"—or words to that effect.

"Marse Kunnel," cried Aunt Ev, "Y' don' wan' t' come in yer! Dis yer 's my place, an' I don' go int' your's. I does m' cookin' m' own way, an' it dun tas'e good. 'F I gits up good vittles y' don' wan' t' see nothin' mo'. Marse Kunnel, I dun sorry y' come dow' yer!"

"But, Aunt Ev, I never can stand this. I'll have to put a stove in here so you can cook easier and have things slicked up."

"Stove!! Marse Kunnel, I nev' cook by no stove. Dunno how. I nev' see stove. Oh, Marse Kunnel, don' put in noth' but d' ole fir'-place I dun cook by fort'-sixt' year."

But I ordered a stove, to which Aunt Ev consented when I told her it must be either a stove or a new cook, and that she must learn to use it. I ordered her, too, to see that things were washed up and kept clean; and that her cooking dishes must be as carefully washed as were those that came on the table. After I had gone out, I thought I heard something about "damned Yanks;" but I paid no attention to it.

The next day, after the new stove had been put up, the house began to fill with smoke; Aunt Ev came tottering to my office, with streaming eyes from the smudge, exclaiming:

"Oh, Marse Kunnel, I dun tol' you d' a stove won' wuk in d' ole fir'-place. See, d' hull house fill w' smudge, an' m' eyes is dun out!"

I went down to the kitchen to see what was the matter, and found she had made the fire in the oven. I showed her where it should be made, and sent a Yankee orderly to superintend the breaking in of the stove.

"I dun s'pose d' fire mus' b' made in d' bigges' place," said Aunt Ev, "an' don' s'pose such lillie fir' kin cook wi' d' hull stove."

Our dinner was late, and burnt. The whole arrangement of the culinary department was broken up; and the result was that we had to surrender, and go back to the old way. But we soon took the field, and Aunt Ev went, too, because she couldn't leave us (and her morning dram of Commissary), and there she cooked by camp-fires.

FORREST AND THE SILVER PISTOL.

You must not think, sir, to catch old birds with chaff.
—Cervantes.

If I can catch him once upon the hip,
I will feed fat the ancient grudge I bear him.
—Merchant of Venice, Act I., Scene 3.

HE COLONEL had his cavalry command in Northern Alabama, where he was mainly hunting guerillas, and especially the men who had murdered Gen. McCook, varied by an occasional brush with parts of the commands of Gens. Forrest and Dick Taylor. One day there came to him a letter, sent through the lines, from Gen. Forrest in which he said he had been credibly informed that when the colonel came upon any of his men he shot them with a silver pistol that he had, and that his shot was always known, for the men were invariably hit in the center of the forehead, and that he had offered a reward of five hundred dollars for the silver pistol and fifteen hundred dollars for the colonel, dead or alive.

For all it seemed like an ugly menace, the colonel sent him a jocular answer with some allusion to "catching a weasel asleep," and dismissed the matter from his mind.

A year or so passed by and neither the colonel nor his famous silver pistol was captured. The war was over and the colonel was commanding a sub-district in Mississippi and acting as a sort of military justice of the peace, while both he and his men were longing and anxiously awaiting an order to go home and be mustered out of the service, when he heard that Gen. Forrest was at one of his plantations not many miles from his headquarters.

Taking a detail of men the colonel started out on an inspection of posts, and at the edge of the evening he drew up at Forrest's mansion. He knocked with the bronze lion-head that was upon the door in lieu of a bell, and the general himself answered the summons, all his negroes having run away long before.

"I understand," said the colonel, "that you have offered a reward of five hundred dollars for Col. ——'s silver pistol and fifteen hundred dollars for the colonel himself. I have brought them both and have come to claim that little two thousand dollars."

The general looked at him for a few moments from under his shaggy eyebrows, while an expression of humor played about his mouth, and then he said:

"I've looked at you often enough through field-glasses. Come in and get a drink."

Gen. Forrest was a man of infinite humor, even with all his dash as a cavalryman and fighter, and the col-

"I've looked at you often enough through a field-glass."

onel always looked back with pleasure on that evening spent with the doughty soldier, as he sat with him enjoying his impromptu hospitality, while his troops were bivouacked outside under the soft summer sky. They talked over their old campaigns, and though there were bitter reminiscences, yet the evening proved to be the cementing of a friendship between them that lasted as long as the general lived.

Long after the war the colonel was called by business to Montgomery, and on Sunday, hearing that vespers were to be sung at the cathedral, he went to hear them. Pew after pew was opened and filled, and he, reaching a pew opened in the broad aisle, was asked to sit at the inner end of it. Soon after Gen. Forrest came up the side aisle and was shown into the pew, just opened, which brought him side by side with the colonel. He bowed to the gentleman who sat immediately in front of the colonel and to the one who sat behind him, and, leaning over to him while waiting for service to begin, he said:

"Colonel, we've got you where we wanted you to be all through the war. You're surrounded by rebels."

Then he introduced the colonel to the gentleman before him, who was Gen. Hardee; and to the one behind him, who was Gen. Johnstone; and after vespers the four took dinner together at a hotel and spent the evening in delightful reminiscence.

One charming characteristic of our American brotherhood is shown in the fact that, however bitter was the animosity and unrelenting the warfare of our "late unpleasantness," when peace was finally declared, old

They spent an evening in delightful reminiscence.

officers and soldiers met in the most amicable way, and if there is hatred now, it is not between those who tested each others' bravery afield, but it is felt only by those who stayed at home, or (strange as it may seem) by those who have come to their manhood and womanhood since the war ended.

COL. DICK MATHER'S LEAP.

'Tis much he dares;
And to that dauntless temper of his mind,
He hath a wisdom that doth guide his valor
To act in safety.—Macbeth, Act III., Scene 1.

In the very May-morn of his youth,
Ripe for exploits and mighty enterprises.
—Henry V., Act I., Scene 2.

COL. DICK MATHER of the —— regiment of —— cavalry was a young dare-devil of a fellow, something on the order of Custer, never dreaming what was the meaning of fear, and, yet, with the coolest head in a scrimmage, even when he seemed to dash in with his men, though it was a forlorn hope. But he came near carrying his hardihood too far one day when he determined to see for himself what was the condition of Forrest's command, down in the southwest. He doubted his scouts, and so, telling his lieutenant-colonel that he would have to be away for a couple of days, and giving him detailed instructions what to do in case he shouldn't be back by the night of the next day, he rode off.

Forrest's command was on the other side of a deep ravine, and only a half-dozen miles from him. Across the ravine, at the upper end of the land that was occupied by Forrest, a trestle-bridge was built so high as to be a giddy place, and with only ties on it for a railroad track. The colonel had reconnoitered it pretty thoroughly from his side, and saw that Forrest had a small picket-post near his end of it. He left directions with his brother, who was just such another reckless, fearless fellow, to be with a couple of horses on the evening of the next day at a thicket not far from his end of the bridge, which he designated, and disappeared.

The next morning a Dutchman came into Forrest's camp, dressed in jeans and wearing a green cap with a broad vizor that shadowed his face, carrying a basket of eggs and butter and such truck, and speaking German and the most broken English. He went all through Forrest's command and even into the general's own tent, selling his dairy products and talking with the men, many of whom were Germans. He was evidently one of their nationality, for he spoke their language as could only a person trained from infancy to it.

He had sold most of the contents of his basket, when he came to the picket near the end of the bridge, with his usual question:

"Vas you buy aigs oder käse?"

They began to chaff him and to mimic his style

of speech, and he received it with good nature and a vacant expression, as though only partly understanding what they said, when one of them pulled up his vizor and, looking him squarely in the face, said:

"You look wonderfully like Col. Dick Mather, and I reckon we'll—"

"Vas you buy some aigs?"

The basket was dashed into his face, filling his eyes with the result of the broken eggs, and two more were struck to earth with his fists, and the colonel—for he it was—sprang over them, and, fleet as a deer, ran for the bridge. From tie to tie he ran, and wondered that they didn't open fire on him. It was soon explained. When he reached the center of the bridge two ties had been taken out! It was a dizzy height, but he ran back half a dozen ties, and getting an impetus for it by his short sprint, he leaped the gap, landing on the tie at the other side. Then they began to fire at him.

By a short sprint he leaped the gap.

Reaching his end of the bridge, he must have swooned, for when he came to himself the Johnnies were just climbing his side of the ravine, evidently supposing he had fallen under their fire, and wanting to secure him, dead or alive.

It was only a short run to where his brother was waiting for him with the horses, and hard riding soon brought them into camp.

Risky? Why it would have been a hopeless and an ignominious death if he had been taken, for no officer would be borne out in leaving his command in that way to turn spy!

Col. Dick, in telling me of it afterward, said:

"One thing I'd like you scientific fellows to explain to me. I'm often, in my dreams, taking that awful leap again, and it seems as if the gap was a mile wide, but I always in my dreams see a cow drinking at the stream, so far down that she don't look bigger than a sheep. But I've no recollection of seeing any cow, or anything, through all that tangle of trestle-work."

POCAHONTAS.

> Heart on her lips, and soul within her eyes,
> Soft as her clime, and sunny as her skies.—Byron.

> What will not woman, gentle woman, dare
> When strong affection stirs her spirit up?—Southey.

I.

IT WAS a wild story of the early part of the war in the far southwest, and I got it from the doctor himself, told as only he can spin a yarn. I'm going to let you have it as he related it, though it must be in cold type and without the glorious flash of his eye and the thrill of his deep baritone voice, and the sudden acting out of parts of it that came involuntarily as he became excited in the narration.

* * * * * * *

Our tent was on a gentle slope not far from the Ozark spring in sunny, sultry Arkansas. The winter was giving way to the warmer airs that presaged the opening summer. Mouse-ear leaves were growing

OLD PARCHMENT.

deeper and broader, and the white flower of the strawberry was making our hearts glad after our long winter's campaign. Missouri seemed to have been conquered. The Confederates had evacuated Springfield and the state; and we, following them south, had buried some of our men and more of theirs at the last fight with their rear guard beyond Sugar Creek.

We were at "Camp Halleck." Below us some fourteen miles lay Fayette, and just beyond, we learned from our scouts, that Price and McCulloch were concentrating their forces for the grand battle that subsequently touched every home in the northwest, and even now causes a thrill in the hearts of the veterans of the southwest at the name of Pea Ridge. The great army of Gen. Curtis stretched out on the prairie and into the woods, the sun glinting on white tents, flashing from bayonets and gun barrels, reflecting from the eagles and bugles of the soldiers' hats, and showing, here and there, the moving masses of troops at battalion drill or on dress-parade; while, wafted on the morning air, there came strains of martial music poured from regimental bands or from the stirring fife and drum.

As I stood on the brow of the little eminence on which my tent was pitched, I was joined by the quartermaster, who gazed with me on the charming scene.

"Ah, Quartermaster," cried I, in my enthusiasm, "isn't it magnificent? See how the whiteness of the tents contrasts with the budding verdure of those old forests, and—"

"Who wouldn't sell his farm and be a soldier!" broke in the jolly man of supplies.

"No, no. But look and listen. How delightful and how inspiring the whole is—"

"What says the poet?"

"'Music hath charms to soothe a savage,
To rend a rock and split a—'

"Never mind, it's too much after the Orpheus style for a quartermaster. Joking aside, I'm going on a forage and the major is going along. Come too. I'll show you fun and secesh."

We were soon mounted and away, over hill and dale, our horses enjoying as much as we the exciting morning coolness.

"You see that house, Doctor," said the quartermaster. "There we'll see 'Beauty and the Beast.' Ask the major."

The major was quite a young man—surely not twenty-five—tall, handsome, with features well defined, but adorned and shaded by a large beard and mustache and wavy locks, all of the most jetty black. His well-fitting uniform displayed to fine advantage the symmetry of his muscular limbs, and as he sat gracefully on his Morgan, I looked at him with unmixed admiration.

"She's a fine girl, Doctor, but she's a little rebel. I think she owes her proclivities merely to her southern birth and education. She comes to see and comfort 'Old Parchment,' as we call her—the old woman who owns this cabin."

"Ah, Major, that tinge on your cheek leads me to suppose you may convert her to Union sentiments," I said rather mischievously.

"Union, egad! the major well might," cried the quartermaster, "for as I'm Q. M. of this regiment, I never saw a handsomer girl—away from home. But judge for yourself."

He sprang from his horse and went into the house and we followed him.

By the side of the fireplace sat "Old Parchment" on a three-legged stool. Her wrinkled, sun-dried and snuff-stained face seemed ready to crinkle and rattle if she moved her mouth, while from her angular body hung soiled and ancient garments—as the quartermaster whispered to me, "like a stocking on a hop-pole." From her toothless jaws there protruded a pine stick like a butcher's skewer, as though, hog and hominy being her sole diet, she chewed the softer implements of the shambles to taste fresh beef. She rose as we entered, and taking from a niche in the fireplace a tin mustard-box, she plunged into it the stick (one end chewed into a little broom), filled it with maccaboy and thrust it into her mouth again.

"Dipping, by the gods!" whispered the quartermaster.

On the opposite side, in all her maiden beauty, sat the antipodes of "Old Parchment," the beautiful girl who had been named Pocahontas by the whole country thereabout. There she was before us, with bright blue eyes, rosy lips and the delicate penciling of dark-brown eyebrows, and long sweeping lashes, over-arched by waves of the most luxuriant hair. Yet there was something about her that made you look at her again. Though now so pensive, there seemed a latent fire in her eyes that might flash forth at some time with an unexpected brilliancy, and on a second look you could discover that peculiar quietude of the lips and mouth, and the gentle dilation of the nostrils that spoke an indomitable energy and an astonishing firmness. The impulse of the masculine in her nature that accompanied your first view of her face was speedily lost as you discovered that all was feminine, but with a reserve that held great strength. Pocahontas was beautiful, but it was the forest beauty, rosy, fresh and rich. She was graceful, but not with the artificial grace of the ball-room; it was the grace of what must be rare physical strength, and the unrestrained play of muscles that could come only to a child of nature. And yet she was cultured, as I found, having spent some years in one of the best southern schools. Now she was again on her native heath and felt the freedom that she was glad to enjoy and to show.

"I'm southern born," she said, "knowing little and caring less for politics, but I think you have no right to come here and free our servants after you have pushed 'Old Lincoln' into the Presidential chair over our heads."

"But, my dear young lady," said I, "we have nothing to do with the negroes, and as for Lincoln, he is no more put into the White House over your head than over mine. I voted for Douglas, so did the quartermaster and so did the major. I cannot consent to secession because, in the due course of the ballot, Lincoln has been elected over Douglas or Bell or Breckenridge. If this was a cause for secession, the North might have seceded from the South because Buchanan was elected over Fremont five years ago."

"But you know that your people fired the first gun, and have been using most barbarous means toward crushing the South."

"At Sumter?" I asked, rather musingly.

"All say you did," said Pocahontas.

"Oh, we-uns know! They's been a tellin' on us that you-uns ravage the wimmin, an' cut off the chillen's ears, an' rob and maurage permiskus," cried "Old Parchment," with a degree of asperity in her raven-like voice, as she adorned her mouth with a fresh "bresh" full of snuff.

"You're safe at least," said the quartermaster, sotto-voce.

"Have you ever heard of its being done?" I inquired.

"Yes, there's them three widders beyant Cassville, which yew men ravaged an' stumped onto, an' kilt, an' yew know it. I heard tell on't yisterday's a week agone. I 'lowed we-uns was all es good es dead when yew-uns come."

"'The three widows' are perfectly unharmed; and, by the way, there go two of them now on their way to Fayette," and I pointed through a hole in the logs which, by way of etiquette, was called "a winder."

"Well, yew Feds is a mean, sneakin', ornery set

anyhow; jest one-hoss. Yew-uns steal, and hook, and lie, and play the divil right smart."

"Whew!" cried the quartermaster.

Pocahontas did not hear, for the major had taken her out of the house and they were sitting on a log under a tree, where she was drinking in the deep bass of his voice as he pictured in glowing terms the perfection of our government, which had been assailed in the acts of secession that had been passed by southern states. The love of country is stronger than people suppose, and I noticed with pleasure the deepening color of Pocahontas' cheeks and the brighter flash of her eyes as her patriotic ardor burst out in its wealth. She had never before heard the northern side of the question; had never realized that the struggle involved the government beneath which we had been reared, and that all the world was to become discouraged in attempts at self-government if our republic failed.

"Old Parchment," meantime, was pouring out her "wials o' wrath" on the devoted head of the quartermaster, who occasionally grunted out an answer to lead her on.

The quartermaster was a queer fellow. Dry, droll, irresistible, he was the life of the regiment. He was small, a little lame, and possessed that class of face that can be contorted into any desired shape till you would suppose it upside down. His hair was very black, and only a small black mustache, like a third eyebrow, adorned his face. He consoled himself in view of his size and lameness by saying he felt honored in being

She was drinking the deep bass of his voice.

the savior of the regiment, for all the field officers chose him to swear at and break their rage on, because he was helpless; and that they did it for every mistake, whether it was made by the hospital steward or sergeant-major or—"any other man." He was entirely destitute of fear, really possessed almost herculean strength, seemed to be indefatigable, and was so efficient that while other regiments in that far southwest lived on fresh bull beef and parched corn, we had good meat and bread.

"Your men are not very brave, madame," said he.

"Yis, they be, though." Her face seemed malicious, if any expression in particular can be considered possible to a drum-head visage. "You-uns 'll find out they be to yer sorrer yit. But ef the men's skeered, the wimmen's right smart o' grit."

"Can you prove that?" asked the quartermaster.

"Wal, ef I look skeered I don't feel it by a heap; an' yit I'm talkin' a power o' secesh, and yew three ossifers a lookin' on and a listenin'."

"Yes, but you'd hide behind your sex if we should undertake to punish you. But, anyhow, I've been hearing you talk on purpose to find evidence against you, that I might send you to St. Louis."

"O Lord a massy! Take a woman a prisoner! I never! I knowed yew-uns was a set o' brutes! O Lord! I hain't done nothin'. I never tuk up no arms. O Lord, Lord!—"

"But Gen. Halleck has issued orders that female spies shall be sent to the military prison. You, a secesh so near camp, are suspected of being a spy, and

your talk shows that you are one. We shall have to
arrest you; but, maybe, on account of your age, they
won't execute you."

"Oh, massy, massy! I won't never say nothin'
agin. Please don't 'rest me. I didn't never mean no
harm; and I've got a right peart o' dinners fer your
men."

"All the worse, Doctor; she gets them in and pumps
them, hey?"

But "Old Parchment" was so effectually terrified
that the quartermaster assured her of protection if she'd
stop secession talk.

"Auntie," said Pocahontas, as she came into the
door, and stood at her full height, "I'm going to be
for the Union from this time on. I've been wrong, and
I'm convinced of it. We poor women have been fools
in talking against our nation. It is a glorious government
and a glorious flag, and—"

"A glorious appeal has been made by a glorious
little woman," cried the major enthusiastically.

Some soldiers coming in, we moved on.

"Pocahontas is going to Fayette this evening. She
lives there," said the major. He had evidently been
deeply impressed by her rare charms.

II.

The bright day was waning, just as the brightest
days will, and as the sun sank below the horizon, and
the trees gathered their shadows into their arms to be
thrown out again at a new dawn, the rich gold that

spread in a broad sheet over the cloudless sky mellowed and softened into the delicate pencilings that not even our greatest masters have been able to catch on their canvas. The twilight of Arkansas is unsurpassed in America.

We had had a long, tedious ride, had filled all our wagons but three, and had been brought back to the Fayette road.

"I think we had better stop in the woods near here, and fill up in the morning," said the quartermaster. "We are twelve miles from cantonment, and I'm simply hanged if I'm going to put these mules much further to-night."

On a forage the quartermaster always had command of a train, if he went; and, as a staff officer, directed the movements of the escorts, even though the soldiers might be commanded by an officer of the line. The major and I were merely guests of the forage party, and acquiesced in the commands of the quartermaster.

"Wagon-master, corral your wagons, unharness and feed. Captain, we'll bivouac here. You'll find a good place for your men on yonder knoll, and there's a spring of clear cold water within twenty yards of you. Throw out a few pickets. Major and Doctor, come with me and I'll show you a scene of surpassing grandeur."

Pensively we rode along with our reins resting on the necks of our horses. Little was said till the quartermaster turned into the woods and brought us to the brow of a hill where, shielded from view by the heavy timber, we could observe objects for a great distance. We were looking for movements on the part of the enemy, and to discover if there were rebel pickets near at hand. Here burst on our view one of those wonderful landscapes that so frequently astonish the traveler in the southwest.

Stretching across the country below us for the distance of several miles was a range of cultivated land—broad plantations flanked with deep forests in which the sober brown of winter was relieved by patches of tender green, and finding a groundwork in sombre mountains that towered to the sky beyond, crowned to their summits by the majestic oak. Scattered here and there were the residences of the planters, with their three-story verandas, their broad red chimneys built from the ground outside the houses; with their neatly whitewashed negro quarters and garden fences, and all shining whiter and more beautiful as their purity was contrasted with the increasing darkness of the scene while the twilight deepened into night. A single thread of silver wound through the whole landscape till it was folded in the embrace of the forest.

"This seems scarcely a time for words," said the major, "but yet how grand. God makes beauty and man defiles it. God lays out peaceful vistas like this and man rends them with heartless war, and casts over the whole the shadow of death, sulphurous and awful. In a few days this very scene on which we gaze may be sanguine with human blood shed by a brother's hand, and yonder beautiful brook may carry the bloody tale on its bosom, while the years to come may associate with what now is so charmingly peaceful, thoughts that are only horrible."

"Yes," said I, "but there may be a benefit in it all, for broad foundations are better if they rest on hard, practical granite. The soft and beautiful alone has never built a nation, for there must be firm nerve, and indomitable courage and will. Bunker Hill, with its view, was doubtless as beautiful as all this that we see before it became a place of thrilling history. Who would exchange it now for what it was?"

"Yes, yes," cried the quartermaster, "the grit of grandfathers can't be proved to be the grit of grandsons unless it is done in the field; and we must needs draw up our curtain, and show England in the pit, and France, Russia and Austria in the first and second tiers and boxes, why, it won't do to sneer at us as soldiers. We shall lose a vast number of brave fellows, though—thousands of 'em."

"Ah, but remember what Kingsley says:

" 'Old forests but perish new seedlings to cherish.' "

As I spoke, a shriek, borne shrill and filled with agony on the air, roused us from our thoughts.

"Gad!" cried the quartermaster. "That's a she squeal! Some girl has seen a snake or a toad. Pick up your horses between your spurs, and let's see."

Like the wind we rode, pistol in hand, dashing through the wood, now dodging a tree-trunk, now ducking quickly beneath a bough, till we reached the road, when once again came the voice in mortal terror.

"Pocahontas!" came from between the white lips of the major. "Ride! ride for your lives!"

What a scene! Struggling between two strong men, her dress torn, her hair disheveled, and vainly endeavoring to scream again beneath the broad palm which the rough soldier held over her mouth, was the lovely girl. A slight cloud of smoke cleared away from before the major, followed by a simultaneous report from my pistol and that of the quartermaster, and a dead soldier lay beside the beautiful Pocahontas, while the other pitched headlong into the brush as he ran, pierced through head and heart by our balls.

"Quartermaster, ride quick and quiet alarm in corral. Three shots is the picket signal. I'll attend to the dear girl."

She had fainted. How beautiful she was, indeed, as she lay so motionless, so white, beneath the growing moonlight.

"Doctor, we must get her away from here before she sees the dead bodies of these infernal ruffians. O God! if we had not been here!"

I aided him in raising her, and we bore her to the roadside. Gradually she opened her eyes, and a sweet smile stole over her innocent face as she looked into the eyes of him who held her.

"Oh, Major, I've had an awful dream. But where am I? O God! it is true! It is no dream!"

"How did it occur? How came you here?"

"You remember the men who came to the house as you left this morning. The old auntie told them I was going to Fayette this evening, and they have waylaid me. Oh, Charlie! thank God! thank God that you were here!" She hid her head on the major's shoulder and wept. He was near doing it, too. It was the first time she had called him by his first name, though he had known her with a growing love ever since we had been in Arkansas.

The quartermaster came back with a guard of mounted men and a guard of infantry. The latter buried the two dead villains, while, accompanied by the former, we three rode on with Pocahontas (whose horse had not run away), and conducted her safely to her father's house. We had a brisk little skirmish on our way back, we thought, probably, with a rebel scouting party—no unusual event—and, tired enough, we slept even in the face of our excitement.

Days dragged along the vast load of ennui that characterizes the dormant cantonment, which, Micawber-like, waited for something to turn up. Nothing can exceed the weariness of camp-life, where we are waiting, waiting, anxious for an enemy, yet merely forming an immense picket. Go to some small junction on an Illinois prairie remote from any town, and look for the train for six or eight hours, and you may understand what are the soldiers' emotions as, day after day, he waits and hopes, with nothing to do, nothing to read, nothing to think of. His gun is burnished till it shines again. His sabre flashes in its brightness. His garments are brushed till they show the depravity of the contractors, as the light shines through their increasing attenuation. But these are the work of a few hours only in each week. He may go through all the movements of the school for the soldier under his captain, or the maneuvers of the battalion under "the Field," but these are merely the machine-work of the army, the forward and backward movement of the piston, or the unending revolution of the regulator, and they seem to add to rather than detract from the monotony of camp-life. Even the arrival of the sutler with a new stock of goods, or the advent of a wagon-train with mail from home, is only for a day or so, and hours seem interminable.

Little could the home-soldier near some large city, or even on the well-cultivated Potomac, appreciate the lonely army in the border country—a vast city of men alone as a mass, alone as integrals of the mass. So much for the lack of woman in her charms. So much for the elucidation of the great problem of camp-vices.

I heard a sermon, preached in Chicago during the war, on the possibility of soldier virtue, drawn from the camp experience of the Israelites en route from Egypt to the Promised Land. I wondered if the contrast might not be a parallel in the ancient and modern experience of nomad life, had the sons of Jacob been deprived of the holy influence of mothers, sisters, wives and fiancés. No wonder our army chaplains found their wheels blocked and their guns spiked, as, away so far from books and papers and good influences, men became demoralized in the face of their greatest exertions!

Under all these circumstances, what wonder is it that a forage-scout, or a reconnoitre of the enemy's position in picket-scout, should have been hailed with delight?

III.

"Doctor," said the quartermaster, "I'm going on a home-scout to-night and don't want the major to go, for reasons of my own. Let Matt throw the saddle on your horse, and come."

The night was dark and stormy. Heavy winds surged and swept through the tree-tops, which seemed to move wearily among the black clouds that rested on them, and made the vast giants of the wood appear like other clouds, pitchy and cruel. At times the thick mist seemed to yield to the gravitation of earth and come down in sulky vapor, to be driven against our faces, cold, penetrating and gloomy. It was a good night for a scout, for we could talk aloud and not be heard by others, and scarcely by each other, and the muffled sound of the horses' feet in the muddy road was only like a softer sob of the storm that surged like the distant surf-roar of the sea.

"There's dirty work afloat, Doctor," said the quartermaster, "and I want to find out what it is. I didn't want the major to come, for it affects Pocahontas; and, while I have every confidence in his judgment, I am afraid he might not be able to keep down. Do you know who the men were that we had the skirmish with the other night, after our adventure with Pocahontas?"

"Why, I suppose they were secesh pickets, hey?"

"No, they were some of those rascally men of the command on our left!"

"Whew! Go on, I'm interested."

"I went over to 'Old Parchment's' house last night, and as I passed the hat-shop—for you must know that the old he-villain that was, was a butternut-hatter—I heard some of those fellows who were holding secret session inside, and up to whose confab I crept to listen, allude to their comrades that we passed over to the Supreme Court for final judgment. It seems that we earthed two men and winged three in the scrimmage. The picket skirmish that has doubled the guards was nothing more than our fight, and you and the major and I figured as rebel pickets. These men know better, though, and as they are afraid of the major and ourselves, they propose to avenge themselves on Pocahontas. Here, fasten your horse under this clump of trees. They meet again to-night in a little house near here. We must find out what we can and block their game."

We proceeded cautiously among the trees for about a quarter of a mile, groping our way with our hands, when we beheld a light issuing from the crannies of a log building.

"Be cautious, Doctor, they probably have a sentinel out," whispered the quartermaster. "You're an old scout; how shall we do?"

"Find where he is, and—silence him."

Very carefully, and on our hands and knees, we crept along. Not a bush cracked, and fortunately the wet leaves prevented their rattling. I put my hand on the quartermaster's shoulder, and we both stopped. Down in a little ditch before us crouched a dark object, about twenty rods from the building. In stretching

"Who goes there?" cried the sentry, standing up.

his neck to discover what it might be the quartermaster's hand rolled on a round stone, throwing him against a bush that crackled under his weight.

"Who goes there?" cried the sentry, starting up.

"Boh!" I exclaimed like a hog in surprise, and, still prone, I whirled round as though terrified. "Ugh! ugh! ugh!" Still I endeavored with flattering success to imitate the "suidae."

The quartermaster, who was a capital bushwhacker and scout, was out of sight in an instant, though I knew he was not far away.

"Ugh! ugh!" grunted I.

"A hog!" muttered the sentinel. "I'll have him."

Softly he stole from his retreat to bayonet the pig. I now stood behind a tree with my sword grasped in my hand and held beside my leg that he might not see its reflection. Any noise would have alarmed the house, and as my sword was very sharp, and I knew how to use it, I had determined to make short work with him. But before he reached me there was a short, quick struggle, a groan, and the sentinel lay insensible.

"Fists are useful even in the army," said the quartermaster at my elbow. "I've almost unjointed my hand. Let's gag the wretch till we come back."

The work was soon done, and we crept onward to the house. Peering through the crannies we could see two of the United States soldiers and three of the butternut gentry engaged in close conversation. A large fire was burning in the stone fireplace, shedding a broad glare over the objects in the room.

The three natives of Arkansas were cast in the same butternut mold that has been used for modeling the whole tribe. Tall, lathy specimens of their genus, they seemed the impersonization of bilious fever, ague and jaundice. Their jeans pantaloons, through which they had thrust their legs too far, hung limp and loose around their shrunken limbs, and the narrow and hollow chest, the sharp, pinched shoulders, and cadaverous face of each told of long residence and terrible struggles as "poor whites" among the diseases incident to the southwest. But in the glitter of their eyes and in the lying expression of their mouths, as they were stretched in a grin, we could detect that which made us grasp our pistols.

The soldiers were of a class that we seldom had in our army—it is to be hoped—deep-dyed scoundrels who would sell army and comrades to gratify their hellish desires. One was a thick-set man with a flattened nose, rough beard and mustache, shaggy and uncombed hair, sharp and wicked eyes that were very close together, and with the expression of a vicious horse, and an entire physique begrimed with dirt. He was certainly the most villainous compound of evil that ever had met my gaze. The other was tall, dark-browed and cruel in appearance, though far from ill-looking. His features were well formed, though showing plainly the evil passions that reeked and burned in his heart.

"That is the fellow they call 'Gabriel,' because he is so unlike an angel and is so bad," whispered the quartermaster in my ear. "Even his company officers are afraid of him. He's the one who is plotting against Pocahontas. We spoilt his game t'other night by killing his demons. We'll try to do it again. Hark!"

"I jest reckon you-uns has got more'n seventeen thousand men," said one of the butternuts.

"No," answered Gabriel, "we have no more than that number. But, one or the other, we want the way opened to get that girl. I'll show you all through the camp when you come if you will tell me when Pocahontas is coming back to see the old woman."

"Treason, by all that's bad!" whispered the quartermaster.

"Wall, I'll come over to-morrer and tell yer," said the man of the secesh who seemed to be spokesman for his party. "I know a right smart o' the gal. She's a —— fine gal and true seedcesh. I thinks a heap on her."

"You must tell me quick and I'll do the rest myself. That's all I want of you. The main army will move to-morrow, and Sigel will be left behind. I heard him say so. Gen. Davis will form the right and Sigel will protect the rear. A murrain on that major and quartermaster and surgeon. I shall get them out of the way." This last he seemed to say in soliloquy.

The quartermaster and I were now fairly startled, for we were in the main army and we knew nothing of this move. The butternuts, by questioning and promising, mixed with much flattery, were working from the soldiers most valuable information of our army's condition and movements.

"They b'aint all right in yonder, be they?" said a

soft voice close behind us. Our two pistols were at the speaker's heart in an instant.

"Lord! don't be skeered, Capting, it's only Jimmie Howe and me," and the bright eyes of "Leather-breeches" showed how he was enjoying the joke of the surprise.

"Leather-breeches," as for some reason he was called, was a Yankee curiosity in his way. Small, dark-skinned, yet handsome in spite of his little pug-nose, he was the soul of fun, a daring, reckless fellow, yet keen and judicious as a scout. Jimmie was a slow-rolling porpoise of a man, yet very cautious, utterly fearless, and possessing a cat-like tread that would have done honor to an ocelot.

"I hearn ye tell the surgeon you was comin', and didn't want the major along, so I s'posed Poka was the up on't. I wound it out o' old Gabriel in yender—he's a sweet specimen of a angel—this mornin' where he was to be, and he telled me he'd punch my head ef I blowed. Ho! let him punch! Cap., ef there's any fun afloat, count me in and Jimmie too."

"Are you mounted, 'Leather-breeches?'" asked the quartermaster.

"I rather guess I am, boss!"

"Doctor, those fellows mustn't carry that news to Price. We can attend to that devil with an archangel's name afterward. Let's do the butternuts to-night.

We had drawn a little from the building during this whispered council, but had only time to dodge into the bushes when the door opened, sending forth a flood of light into the darkness, but fortunately not falling on the bound sentry, and Gabriel and his companion came out. We could hear them calling their comrade, and supposing him gone, treading roughly through the crackling brush. We got back to the building in time to hear one of the Johnnies say:

"I say, Bill, we've got a right smart o' news outen them fellers. Lots that big chap'll have outen old Cummin's gal. I'm kinder sneakin' arter her myself. The ole man owes me fer work I done fer him, and I git in an' dun him now'n then so's to git sight on her. She kain't go me, shore, with her stuck-up notions, but I'll tame her in. I haven't saw her, though, last week's three month."

"Ki, yew air cute!" laughed Bill as he shrugged his shoulders.

"We'll release old Cummings of that obligation," said the quartermaster in an undertone. "Come on, boys."

We opened the door and went in. "Leather-breeches" and Jimmie followed us.

"You are arrested in the name of the United States Government. Resist at your peril," said the quartermaster.

They had started up and stood gazing at us, but seeing we were evidently alone, their fear seemed to subside in part, for the man who had just spoken to Bill, and who was evidently their leader, exclaimed:

"What in —— do you arrest us fer? We're peaceful citizens. Anyhow we're ekal to you-uns."

"I arrest you as spies," replied the quartermaster

calmly. "If you move toward resistance I won't be answerable for the consequences to you."

The man they called Bill stepped toward the corner where a long Mississippi rifle leaned against the wall, while the other two drew their bowie-knives, but as they sprang forward we fired our pistols. "Leather-breeches" missed his man and only two were dead, but the third dropped from the quartermaster's second ball, just as his keen blade laid open the crimson flesh of Jimmie's arm. The wound was not a bad one, and I bound it with a bandage torn from my own linen.

IV.

The next morning we were ordered to prepare for a march to Pea Ridge, but, as the rascally Gabriel had said, "Gen. Sigel's division was left behind. The major, however, had, as he supposed, silenced all danger from this villain by warning Pocahontas. Rumors followed us rapidly of Price's increasing army, of the arrival of Van Dorn, McIntosh and Slack with reinforcements at Boston Mountains, and of a projected attack. Suddenly the distant boom of cannon announced the battle begun near Bentonville. Sigel was attacked and his train was in danger; with one regiment he was surrounded by ten thousand of the enemy.

Past us dashed Bowen's battery of mountain-howitzers, little toy-like guns on their funnier mules; and down came the cavalry, tearing by to relieve the favorite general. Rifle-pits were dug, ramparts were thrown up, and impediments were cast, by order of the commanding general, in the way of possible cavalry charges, and all on a part of the field where the enemy had no idea of appearing; for, insane as the rebels might be, they would not be guilty of such folly as to expose themselves in an open valley where masked batteries and covered columns of men would have a free course upon them. Sigel fought his way out, thanks to the diversion made, but through the night following the enemy worked around us till we were flanked completely, and by morning our retreat was cut off, our trains were separated from us, and the enemy were thirty thousand strong between us and Springfield!

With the opening dawn commenced the terrible work of death. The loud roar of the batteries echoed from Elk Horn Tavern to Leesburg, responding to each other's hoarse voice, telling of death, of pain, of days and weeks of agony, and of months of anxiety, years of grief, gray hairs brought in sorrow to the grave, and bright locks bleached beneath the scorching glare of agony, at home. The rattle of musketry drowned the death-rattle, and deep graves were plowed by the ricochetting balls, as though in mockery of the poor fellows who would never be buried.

But why portray the horrid scene which has been so vividly pictured by able pens and so truly daguerreotyped on the affectionate hearts that were bereaved? The three-days' battle closed when the week ended, and the Sabbath sun looked down on our field of victory—a field of death. The dead lay thickly strewn over the ground, in some cases lying as they fell, and in others showing how fearful their agony had been, as they had torn up the ground and lacerated their hands in their death struggles. Now all was quiet, save where a wounded man would break the stillness of the air by "the battlefield-groan"—a groan that seemed the concentration of pain, despair and longing for home, in one bundle of agony.

Our army was moved back to the vicinity of Bentonville, though not to the same camping-ground as before.

"Major," said the quartermaster, "'Leather-breeches' has discovered a rough plot that is to be executed to-night. Pocahontas has come back to 'Old Parchment's' and Gabriel has determined to carry her off immediately. 'Leather-breeches' has gone over to warn her. Let's go."

The night was again dark, moonless and cloudy, when we took our position near the house. In the bustle of the battle, impending and present, Gabriel as an informant had been forgotten, and he was still at large. The major was determined on his death, but he wanted to give him opportunity to commit himself before he killed him.

"They're in the house, by the gods!"

We could plainly hear, through the open door, the voice of the savage fellow. He was talking to "Old Parchment."

"Tell me where she is, or by all that's holy, I'll hang you to one of your own house-beams. I don't care if you are a woman, I'll rip out your heart," and there followed a succession of horrid oaths, such as had accented all he had said. Little "Old Parchment" stood her ground well.

"He's fierce, but the bird has flown. Ha! ha!" quietly laughed the quartermaster.

"Egad! there she is!" said the major, almost breathless.

"So, so!" said she calmly as she entered the house by a back door. "You'll hang auntie, will you? What a cowardly bully, to be frightening a poor woman out of her wits! Ah, ha! You're afraid of a little body like me, are you?"

He had, indeed, fallen back and stood gazing at her with mixed wonder and awe. But, suddenly springing forward, he seized her in his arms. We dashed from our covert, but were too late to secure the honor of saving her; she had saved herself. A sharp stiletto had pierced the wicked heart, and the ruffian was thrown from her, but not till his hot blood had spouted upon her dress, staining her white bosom. A sharp skirmish with the remaining fellows followed, and it was not till we bore marks of blood that we stood victors.

Gabriel was dead, and killed by a woman. How her eyes flashed, and how firm were her lips now; how strongly and clearly defined the dilation of her nostrils as, in woman's rage, she contemplated the man who had dared to assault her!

"Saved again, and saved by you, dear Charlie. I know it isn't womanly, but I can't help it. If I had a dozen such men against me it seems as though I could defeat them to-night. 'Leather-breeches,' God bless you. You're a dear, good boy," and she kissed him kindly.

"Now, Pocahontas, what will you do?" said the major. "I can't bear to leave you alone, exposed to such dangers. Why all should fall on you I don't know, and yet my heart tells me why." He spoke very musingly.

"Charlie, you mustn't become romantic now. I have other things to speak of." Pocahontas was kind and even affectionate in saying this, but yet she was firm. "There's a regiment of Missourians that will disband in a few days, and I think you can secure their guns. Price is going towards the river, and perhaps to Tennessee. These troops won't go."

"Where will they be?" asked the major.

"They will probably be at 'Cow-pen Cave.' If I can find out when they break up I'll guide you to it."

"You!"

"Yes, I. If I can coax 'Leather-breeches' to bring me your dagger," showing the major's beautiful stiletto, "and can kill that dog, I can ride as guide with you."

Her eyes were soft, serene and affectionate now as she looked ingenuously into the major's face. The human heart is so strange a thing; one hour fierce and flashing angrily from the eyes—those windows of the soul—and the next soft, subdued and full of love.

"She's a strange woman, that Pocahontas," said the quartermaster, as we were aiding "Leather-breeches" and Jimmie to bury the dead.

"Yes, but she's noble," said I.

"A blessed, blessed girl," said the enthusiastic and adoring young major.

V.

Dark, heavy clouds were rolling and crashing against each other just above the horizon, and the perfect stillness of the evening air seemed to portend a terrible tempest. The thunder grew more and more loud as the clouds, which at first had been lying in huge banks of silver resting on a coal-like base, had now finally obscured the sun, and the darkness had stolen up their vast masses, pushing up the brightness till it was all gone, and had become a pitchy black. The wind broke out with great fury, surging and swaying our tents, and growing louder and louder in its roar, till it shook the giants of the forest. Angry drops of rain were dashed against the tent, and every moment came faster and heavier, while the deep thunder reverberated among the hills and rolled through the valleys around us, as though the Great Ruler would show his creatures how much more fearful his artillery was than theirs of a few days before.

In the midst of it all the quartermaster rode up and, springing from his horse, threw himself on the tent-cot.

"I've had a long ride—forty miles out and back since four o'clock this morning. But I've found those guns. They are at Cow-pen Cave, and we can get them. I saw Pocahontas and she said she should be here this evening. Any other woman would be far from venturing out on such a night. God! there she is!"

"Come, be quick. They are going to take the guns away," said she as she came in. Pocahontas was dressed in a riding habit of water-proof cloth, with an india-rubber poncho on her shoulders, while her head was covered with a broad-brimmed and closely-plaited sombrero.

"How many guns are there, and how are they guarded?" asked the major.

"Nine hundred and sixty-odd guns, guarded by about a hundred and fifty men," said Pocahontas.

"Adjutant, detail Company I, and quartermaster, let the wagon-master bring round four wagons immediately. You may take charge of the expedition. Doctor, get your case, and we will go too."

The major and Pocahontas rode before, then the quartermaster and I, followed by the men and wagons. The rain came down in sheets upon us, and seemed to run in rivers along the road. The darkness was fearful, but Pocahontas was unerring as a guide. Over high hills and through deep valleys we marched, a slow and tedious journey, through swollen creeks, till all were drenched, the men keeping up good spirits in view of a skirmish, and surmounting every difficulty by saying: "We can go anywhere that she can!"

Toward morning the party was brought to a halt, for we were near the cave. There was no danger of our being heard, for the heavy thunder still rolled with terrific violence. That storm we have always remembered as the "all night thunder-shower!"

"You'd better throw out skirmishers and surround the cave. You'll have to fight, I promise you," said Pocahontas.

A few moments afterward the sharp crack of a rifle carried us all to the immediate vicinity of the cave-mouth, where we met the enemy, the lightning revealing their position. The parties must have been nearly equal, and the fight, by the light of the lightning, was a severe one. The voice of the valiant quartermaster could be heard between the peals of thunder, till the enemy was driven from the field. Then he cried:

"Forward! Seize the guns! Wagon-master, bring up the transportation."

As the light of our flambeaux flashed upon the distant part of the room we entered, we were lost in wonder and admiration. Stalagmites and stalactites, shimmering under the light cast upon them, seemed to be vast jewels—a cave of diamonds! While the men were securing the guns that lay in heaps on the floor, the quartermaster and I pushed on to the next room in hope of finding more. In the center of the hall stood a tall figure, like some old Roman with his toga wrapped around him. We started at first and grasped our pistols, but we laughed a moment afterwards as we saw it was formed of the beautiful aqueous stone—the hardened droppings of centuries. We could not penetrate further, for we had missed the major and Pocahontas, and asked each other where they were, and if any of the men were wounded.

No one had seen them. We went with our flambeaux searching, calling. Suddenly a moan was heard, and running thither, we beheld the beautiful Pocahontas lying partly across the prostrate body of our noble friend. She shed no tears, but her pale face was deathlike as the glare of our torches revealed it.

"O God!" she moaned. "Let me die, too! Let me die, too!"

We raised her gently and I examined the wound.

"Is he dead?" asked the quartermaster.

"No, only fainted."

"O Doctor, for God's sake bring him back. Dear Doctor, do save him!" Now she wept.

It was a severe wound, but not dangerous. He must have been shot in the early part of the engagement and had now merely fainted from loss of blood. He had fought on, even when he was so badly hurt, for we had seen him in the thick of the skirmish till toward the close of it.

"Pocahontas, he isn't in danger. The wound is not so bad. He will revive soon." I put to his lips a flask of diluted spirits that I always carry to the field for such a purpose, and soon he opened his eyes and smiled to the dear girl who hung over him.

"Oh, God be praised! God be praised! Dear Charlie, speak to me. You will get well. O God! if you should die!" She made no secret of her love. It was the genuine outburst of nature.

"Dear Pocahontas, will you take care of me till I'm well?"

"Indeed I will, Charlie."

"And always afterwards?"

POCAHONTAS NURSING THE MAJOR.

"Yes, Charlie." Her hand clasped his. He tried to take it with the other also, but it fell helpless. His arm was shattered.

We carried him back on an impromptu bed made in one of the wagons, the lovely Pocahontas riding by the side of him. The night was gone, but still the heavy rain poured in pitiless volumes, and Pocahontas had covered the major with her poncho. A dozen blankets were tendered her by the men, but, no! her poncho must be over the wounded man.

"Pocahontas," asked the major, as I dressed his broken limb after we had returned, "what if I should lose my arm; would you love me still?"

"Would you have loved me if I had lost mine instead? I had as good a chance to as you did.''

"Indeed I would."

"Then you can answer your question for yourself. Why, Charlie, I'd love you anyhow."

"Yes, Doctor," said the major, "she rode by me through the whole fight, though I didn't let her know when I was hit. The balls were flying like hail, and still there she was. I thank God that I entered the army—I've got a noble treasure by it."

"I'm thankful, too," murmured Pocahontas.

Day after day and night after night did the sweet girl sit by him in untiring devotion, bearing with him if the long, restless nights made him fretful, fanning him in the heat of the day, pouring cold water on the angry wound, and giving up her place only to the quartermaster or "Leather-breeches" or "Dr. Ed," as she called me.

Among the other wounded men, too, she was the angel of hope, and her name was on their lips with blessing.

* * * * * * *

I was called away. The major's arm was nearly well. And as, after two months' absence, I returned, I found myself received with a cordial welcome in the major's well-furnished marquee. Pocahontas came and sat by me while her husband—still the same young hero—had gone to dress parade.

"I love you, too, Dr. Ed," said Pocahontas. "You saved Charlie's arm."

BRAVERY.

O friends, be men; so act that none may feel
Ashamed to meet the eyes of other men.
Think each one of his children and his wife,
His home, his parents, living yet or dead.
For them, the absent ones, I supplicate,
And bid you rally here, and scorn to fly!
—Bryant's Homer's Iliad.

Tender handed stroke the nettle,
  And it stings you for your pains;
Grasp it like a man of mettle,
  And it soft as silk remains.—Aaron Hill.

HE QUESTION is often asked a soldier if he was afraid before he went into battle and how he overcame his timidity; and, also, if the excitement and enthusiasm of a battle enabled him to forget himself and lose his fear. It is said that at one time, when the Duke of Wellington was looking over a regiment before it was ordered into a fight, one of his aids pointed to a man who stood pale and trembling in the ranks, and said:

"Your grace, there is a man who is a coward."

The Iron Duke looked at the man and replied:

"He's the bravest man I see, for he knows his danger, but he faces it."

I had a young fellow in my headquarters one evening before a fight—a sort of pet of mine and of a family I well knew and loved at home, who said:

"I'm afraid I'll be afraid, but I won't be, if I die for it;" and he wasn't.

It is said that an old Scotch soldier cried out in the heat of a heavy fight:

"Sandy, I'm 'feared we'll all be kilt afore we win."

In one of our battles, when twenty-eight men of Company A fell in the first volley, and when it looked like the annihilation of our command, a soldier turned to me as he was slipping a cartridge into his gun, and said:

"A fellow has only to open his mouth to catch it full of bullets!"

But men are afraid, and the more sensitive is the nerve of the man the more sure he is to be. I had in my command a lad whom I well knew and whose parents and sisters were among my intimate friends at home, who came into my tent one evening before we were starting out for what proved to be a serious battle, and he said:

"Won't you excuse me to-morrow and let me stay back with the baggage-train? I know I'll be afraid and will disgrace my family. I can't bear that they should hear of my showing the white feather on the field."

I told him that he shouldn't show it, and that his

mother and sisters should never hear of any such disgraceful thing, for I would have two men behind him with orders to shoot him dead if he undertook to run

But he went afield next day with two hard-eyed fellows beside him.

away, and all his people would know was that he fell on the field.

The poor fellow fairly grovelled on the floor of my tent, and wept and prayed me, in a very paroxysm of terror. But he went afield the next day, and with two hard-eyed fellows by him who he felt sure would carry out the orders he supposed them to have from me. Through that day he was the bravest and coolest of all, and afterward he thanked me for holding him to his duty, for he said that he soon forgot his fear, and, anyhow, hadn't as much as he thought he was going to have. He came out of the war with two bars on his shoulder-straps.

A colonel tells me that the captain of Company A, in his regiment of cavalry, showed signs of fear to such a degree that he would "turn white about the gills," and his knees would almost smite together when he was going into a fight. The colonel thought it was necessary to give him a severe test, for that was his best company, so one day, in a hot fight, he said:

"Captain, I want you to dismount your men, leave every fourth man with the horses, deploy your men as skirmishers (at a place which he pointed out), and hold that point till I relieve you if it costs you every man of your company. It is a most important service, and I won't keep you there any longer than I can help. Are you equal to it?"

The captain had a lump in his throat and could hardly reply. It was pitiable. But he chokingly said:

"Y-e-s, sir. Lieutenant, order up the men."

Awhile after the colonel rode down to where they were—and it was hot—and found the men lying on their faces and occasionally popping at the enemy, while the captain stood leaning against a tree, whittling a bit of stick that he held in his hand as though it was a lead pencil which he was sharpening. He was not

The captain stood leaning against a tree whittling a bit of stick.

behind the tree. Hearing the click of the horse's foot against the stones, he looked over his shoulder, and seeing the colonel, said, coolly enough:

"Don't you think you'd better get off your horse and hide behind a stump?"

"For what?" asked the colonel.

"Then I'd have an excuse to do it, too."

Just then a bullet struck the tree over his head, and looking up, as calmly as if he had been in his own lumber-yard at home, he said.

"You see, sir, that they come—close sometimes."

The colonel said: "I'm about to relieve you and your men, Major—"

"What's that you called me, sir?" cried he.

"I called you major. You know there's a vacancy in the third majority of our regiment; and as soon as I can get a commission from the Governor of our state, your name will be in it."

"What does that mean, sir? I——"

"Bravery on the field, Major."

"Oh, my God!" he cried with intense emotion, "I just want to live long enough to write it home to Susie!"

The major (for he got his commission in due time) afterward confessed to the colonel that he had been afraid, most miserably and morbidly afraid, but when he got down there and saw his men—sixteen-dollar a month men and with no hope of promotion, but with hard quarters, hard fare, hard labor—saw them brave, enduring and for patriotism, somehow a change came over him, he could not tell how, and all sense of fear left him.

QUANTRELL.

> The oppressive, sturdy, man-destroying villains,
> Who ravaged kingdoms, and laid empires waste,
> And in a cruel wantonness of power,
> Thinned states of half their people, and gave up
> To want the rest.—Blair.
>   So spake the seraph Abdiel, faithful found,
>   Among the faithless, faithful only he.—Milton.

HE CAPTAIN told me the story himself. He had been all through the "border-ruffian" war in Kansas, and had exchanged shots once with Quantrell himself, the arch-ruffian putting a bullet through his arm, and he missing—he could not tell how, for he did not often miss—and only making a hole in Quantrell's hat. Quantrell shouted back:

"If I ever get you, you'll hang at sunrise!"

The captain thought that was a game at which two could play; but he was determined, if any hanging was done, it shouldn't be he.

The Kansas war was over and was successful for the Union and abolition side. Slavery had had its

Bushwhackers waiting for the enemy.

bounds proclaimed, and out of it had grown the great war that was to remove even those bounds by doing away with slavery itself. In the early part of that war the captain was in Missouri and still on the same side. One day he went out to carry some medicine to a soldier who was hidden in the house of a Union family. The poor fellow had been wounded in a guerilla fight, shot by a "bush-whacker" in a brush that the captain's company had with them, and was too badly hurt to be moved. The warm-hearted captain, who loved his men, got out to him occasionally; but it was very risky, for a bush-whacker is a soldier one hour, and the next is innocently plowing his field with the horse he has been riding, while his saddle and gun are hidden under some weeds in a fence-corner. They never wore any uniform but their "jeans."

There was a sudden rush from the underbrush, and, though the captain fought as hard as he could, he was overcome by numbers, was knocked down, his hands were tied behind him, and he was a prisoner. They put him on his horse again, and after a couple of miles ride, he found himself in a dusky dell in mid-woods in the presence of—Quantrell!

He saw that recognition was mutual and immediate, for a revengeful scowl settled on the face of the notorious bandit, and he said, fairly between his teeth:

"So, ho, my rum cove, the innings are mine. You pay for my hat with your head, as I promised you. So help me God, you hang at sun-up."

The captain was a cool, determined man, and however he might feel that he had met his fate, the Kansas butcher of women and children should not see it. He merely said:

"If I am here."

"I've almost a mind to put a bullet through your —— head."

"You will be here," shouted Quantrell, enraged that his victim was so self-possessed and confident. "Strap his arms and his legs, and stake him down in a pup-tent, and we'll see if he is here. I know how to hold a man when I get him. You—hang—at sunrise!" All this was interlarded with nearly as many brutal oaths as there were words in the sentences.

Stakes were driven into the ground in a wedge-tent, and with his hands tightly tied and his feet also, the captain was fastened to the stakes so that he could hardly move as he lay upon the ground. The vicious face of the bandit-chief was over him all the time, gloating over his capture. He said:

"I've almost a mind to put a bullet through your —— head; but hang it is, hang, hang!"

The evening settled into a night of pitchy darkness. Not a ray of light penetrated the little tent, and the captain strove to release himself from his bonds. His hands were small, even if they were sinewy, but the ropes were tied too tightly. While he lay there, a prey to thoughts far from enviable, he heard a slight rustle at his back, and then breathing close to his ear. The sensation was horrible. He expected a knife to be thrust between his ribs at any moment. The fell ruffian was equal to any revenge of assassination, and might resort to it in fear of the escape of his prisoner, whom he knew to be an experienced scout. But, instead, there came a whisper in most undeniable dialect:

"Marster, don' make no noise. Show me whar' yo' hands is."

A knife was sawing away at the cords that bound his hands—what did the captain care if it cut a deep gash into his thumb joint—and, with hands set free, he took the knife and cut loose his feet. Then came the same whisper, scarcely above a breath:

"Marse, now put yo' hand on my heel, and crawl."

The "crawl" seemed to be for miles and for hours, but at last the negro said aloud:

"Now, git up and we'll walk."

After several miles of walking, with never a word from the negro, and through darkness that the captain said was "black as tar," the negro said:

"Now, marse, we's done crawl again."

Again came a long and slow progress on hands and knees, the black man often grunting like a pig, and once more he rose and said:

"Now, marse, yo's inside de Union lines and cyarn't git out nohow!" and he disappeared into the black night.

The captain, groping about, soon heard the familiar challenge, "Who goes there?" and giving the reply, found himself in the midst of his own company. But of his black preserver he never heard. Whether he was detected and was slain by the angry free-booter, or why he went back at all without allowing himself to be known in the Union camp, he never could learn. Yet it was all of a piece with what was always to be found of that enigmatic race of faithful men, who never were to be doubted by our Union men, and yet held a dog-like attachment to their own former masters.

CAUGHT AGAIN.

Upon the next tree thou shalt hang alive,
Till famine cling thee.—Macbeth, Act V, Sc. 5.

The better part of valor is discretion; in the which better part I have saved my life.—Henry IV, Pt. I, Act V, Sc. 4.

HERE was a worse and harder test for the brave Captain with this awful Quantrell. A number of his men who had been wounded were hidden among the people friendly to the Union. These kind people that made hospitals of their homes were noble, self-sacrificing souls, who, though they were not in the army, yet were willing to do what they could, by receiving and caring for poor fellows when they were wounded or sick. They would hide away the soldiers' clothes which would have betrayed them; and nursed them as though members of their families; often saying, when examined as to who they had in the house, that the sick man was a son or brother. It was seldom that they could not lie out of their danger.

Is such a lie a sin? Ah! think how it is squeezed out by very pity and love! Might we say of it as of the oath in Tristram Shandy, "The accusing spirit, which flew up to heaven's chancery with the oath, blushed as he gave it in; and the recording angel as he wrote it down dropped a tear upon the word and blotted it out forever." Think of our loved and lamented Whittier's words:

> "Hope not the cure of sin till self is dead;
> Forget it in love's service, and the debt
> Thou can'st not pay the angels shall forget;
> Heaven's gate is shut to him who comes alone;
> Save thou a soul, and it shall save thine own."

The Captain was very tender of the men who were so being cared for; carrying them medicines and any delicacy they might need. The Colonel protested that it was a dangerous thing for him to do; and especially after his narrow escape from the bold and relentless guerrilla chief. But now word had come from the scouts that Quantrell and his gang were gone to Arkansas, and the Captain felt that he could safely look after one of his men who was very ill at the house of a German farmer, and who was in great need of an opiate. So he started for him with some opium in his pocket.

There was a dash at him by half a dozen men. Two of them he knocked down, but he was overpowered, his legs were tied beneath his horse, and he was taken to the guerrilla camp, where he found himself standing again before the awful freebooter, Quantrell! The scouts had been mistaken.

"Ha! ha! my Daisy. I've got you again, hey? You see you were born for the halter,—if I don't sock an ounce of lead into you too soon. You got away before. Now you are my meat! Maybe you think you can play that game twice. But I know a trick worth two of that. So, look at the sun, for you'll never see it again. I'll hang you 'to a sour apple tree' before it can get up high enough for you to see. Ho! ho!"

Calling two of his men he told them to lay the Captain between them, and see that he was there in the morning; assuring them, with many oaths, that if he was gone, they'd hang in his place.

He was carried to a tent, and the savage, eagle eyes of his guards were upon him. Time dragged on heavily until it grew dark, but at last he said:

"Say, fellows, if I was guarding you, and you were to be strung up in the morning, I don't believe I'd let you lie and think about it all night if there was any whiskey to be got, so a fellow could have a good, roaring drink to put him to sleep."

"Say, Bill, if he was drunk enough we could keep him all the closter," said one of them.

"I don't object none," said the other. "Tom Fagan has got a canteen of Commissary. Git it."

While this ruffian was gone for the "moisture" the Captain managed to get into the palm of his hand the full dose of opium from his pocket; and when it came, he took the canteen and as he held it, with a hand at the uncorked neck, and shook it to get the drug into it, he said:

"Don't it sound good, slashin' away in the old tin!

Just think what drunks are in it, and it so small. Here's sleep and don't care. Here's doing away with thinking. Boys, here's to you, and better luck than seems to come for me."

With the "medicine" well mixed, he put the canteen to his lips, and setting his tongue into the nozzle, he seemed to drink, and tried to make it sound as if the whiskey was gurgling down his throat. Then he coughed as though it had strangled him, making some of the liquor fly from his mouth as if he had choked with a mouth full.

Handing it to the man on his right, it did him good to hear him swallow it. Every gulp of it seemed like life to the Captain. Then after taking another drink (apparently) himself, he passed it to the other man; but as he listened in intensest interest to his drinking he suspected that he followed his own ruse and only seemed to drink; no doubt suspecting that the Captain wanted to make him drunk, but having no suspicion of the drug:—for even bitter opium can't make Commissary whiskey taste worse.

They finished the canteen, our Captain managing to spill enough to answer for what he was supposed to have taken, and after a while it began to tell on them all. The two men fell asleep and the Captain feigned a heavy drunken stupor. The man on his right was snoring, and the Captain managed to get from his sheath a large bowie-knife, but without appearing to move. He was cool and level-headed, as he was utterly fearless, as I said in the other story of Quantrell, and an old scout—not in years, but in experience—and could do such a thing with the skill of a prestidigitator.

When both of his guards seemed lost in profound slumber, the Captain, by digging his heels in the ground was working his body up from between his drunken guardians, and had got his knees on a level with their heads, when the man on his left clapped his hand on him and said:

"No, you don't!"

"It appeared to me," said the Captain, when he told me about it, "as if all the blood in my body was in my head, and yet I seemed to have the strength of a giant. It was a short, sudden blow with the bowie as it went, true as fate, to his heart, and was plunged in so deep that the hilt struck his ribs. He didn't utter a sound, but just a gasp, and there he lay. He had feigned the whole—drink and sleep and all; and the other fellow must have been about dead from the opium he had swallowed. No one could ever have wakened him again, and I don't believe they hung him."

The night was dark, especially in the thick woods, as the Captain crept out of the tent and into a thicket. By the aid of the undergrowth, and with the instinct of an Indian, he crept from bush to bush, avoiding sentries, as he well could by his keen sight and hearing, till he got out of the camp.

It was far from being safe yet, for roving parties of guerrillas were all about. But he knew the country, even to the very paths in the woods; and by never letting up on his vigilance, hiding in the underbrush on the slightest noise, it must be lynx-eyes and the ears of a fox that could detect him. Before morning he heard the well-known and gladly answered challenge of one of his own sentinels.

Whenever he went to visit his sick men after that, he always took with him a body-guard, for he said:

" 'Three times and out'—of the world!"

THE SABRE-TEST.

All the gods go with you! Upon your sword
Sit laurel victory, and smooth success
Be strewed before your feet.
—Antony and Cleopatra, Act I., Scene 3.

Recollection is the only paradise from which we cannot be turned out.—Richter.

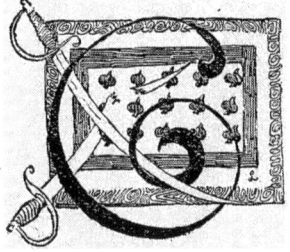

COL. NAGELEY of the —— regiment of —— cavalry was waited upon by a couple of lieutenants one day who told him that several of them wanted to buy a sabre for presentation to a friend of theirs who was a cavalry officer, and that they ventured to ask him to test and select a blade for them, as they knew he was a connoisseur in all matters of arms. The colonel was a good-natured man, and maybe he was susceptible to this delicate bit of flattery, so he went with them to the armorer's, and calling for "the best that was to be had," he proceeded to give them severe tests, and especially one that he had seen applied somewhere abroad. Three blades broke under his hand, and he said to the dealer:

"If you want me to break up your stock keep on bringing me sabres with flaws in them. A sabre for active service, and where a life may be dependent on it, wants to be able to endure any test."

Saying that the method of testing which had broken

He advised the officers to get it, expensive as it was.

the ones that had failed was new to him, and he had never seen it applied before, the dealer brought a blade that he was sure would endure any handling.

"I don't expect," said the colonel, "to find a Ferara or a Toledo blade."

"And you don't need to do so," said the armorer, "for there are as good blades made to-day as the old Ferara of the sixteenth century and Scotland; and certainly our country can turn out as good work as Toledo, in Spain, or any other nation. It is a pity if we can teach the world everything besides and not surpass in that as well. Here is a blade that is hand-made, as all swords should be, and the tempering is as perfect as it can be, and it was in water and not in oil. You may try your best on it, sir, in side or edge or point stroke, and even your new and awful way."

The sabre came out unscathed from beneath the colonel's brawny arm, and he advised the officers to get it, expensive as it was. With that he left them that they might give directions to the armorer, and the whole affair passed out of his mind.

A week later the colonel was surprised, as he sat in his tent after dress-parade, to see the line officers of the regiment march up and form under the fly which was stretched before his headquarters, and, with the captain of Company A as spokesman, to have presented to him the very sabre he had selected, richly mounted and in a heavy bronze scabbard on which was a silver plate duly inscribed. It was presented to him by his company officers.

"We were very grateful to you for falling into our scheme and selecting your own sabre," said the captain of Company A, "for now we know you have one that you can trust, and so can we. We hope it will carry you through all the war, and that you will have it to hang up at home 'when this cruel war is over,' as a remembrance of your officers; while we pledge you that wherever that sabre flashes we will follow."

The colonel was completely taken aback, for he had not for a moment suspected that it was for himself

It was presented to him by his company officers.

he was testing a blade; but he assured his officers of the gratification he felt, and said he would make no pledges to them for its use till all was over, and then they would need none. He told them of his pride in his command, and that, though he had not tried his men under fire, he was sure they would stand as well as had this blade, the heaviest tests that could be put upon them, and he would try to stand by them in their battles and not run away. So went on a charming evening of chat, in which the field officers joined.

That sabre was not disgraced during the service, and now, more than thirty years later, the old sabre, with blade and scabbard silver-plated to keep it from rust, is hanging in the sitting-room of the colonel's daughter, who prides herself on having heroic blood in her veins, which every dent on that old blade and its scabbard endorses.

Many of the old officers of that regiment are dead—some afield and some since—but the venerable colonel, who still lives, insists upon it that they live too; not as bare pictures on the walls of his memory or as statues in its niches, but as they were on that day of the presentation, alive, young, active, and the bravest lot of men that he ever knew.

THE NEW GENERATION.

O, withered is the garland of the war,
The soldier's pole is fallen.
—Antony and Cleopatra.

He was not merely a chip of the old block, but the old block itself.—Burke.

I WAS quite startled a few years ago in being called upon by the principal of the high school at Toledo, Ohio, to give a talk to his graduating class on the war and on slavery, as he said he had just realized that every member of the class had been born since the war closed and since slavery had ceased. He thought our war was to those young people about what the war of 1812 had been to me when I was a boy. I gave the address with a sort of sense of depression in thought that I was growing old—was a veteran, indeed—and that a new generation was coming on who were to crowd us off the stage of action.

A few days afterwards I met Gen. Steedman, whom we called the old "War-horse of Chickamauga," and I told him of the strange sense that had come to me. He said:

"I had the same shock a few days ago, for I had some old officers dining with me, and we were talking over the old war times, when my thirteen-year-old

"Which side were you on, grandfather?"

granddaughter looked up to me and asked: 'Which side were you on, grandfather?' Ye gods!"

At the dedication of the soldiers' monument on East Rock, at New Haven, in Connecticut, I chanced to be on the reviewing stand with Gen. Sherman, Gen. Sheridan, Gen. Terry, Gen. Hawley and other distinguished officers, while the great procession marched by. The crowd was dense, the day was hot, the delays had been long and frequent, it was past the dinner hour, and the veterans of that immense column were getting old, and were tired and hungry and faint. Now and then a shout went up for "Uncle Billy" or

I chanced to be on the reviewing stand with Sherman.

for "Little Phil," or for one of the loved and honored Connecticut generals, but it was half-hearted and the attempt at an old army yell was a failure.

After they had passed by came the column of the "Sons of Veterans," with young men, lithe, active, straight as arrows, and as they were told who were the great generals on the stand, the caps were tossed up, and their yells were given in a way that reminded us of days of auld lang syne. All at once Gen. Terry, our lamented Connecticut hero, turned to Gen. Sherman and said:

"Those old fellows who have just gone by weren't the men who saved the country. It was just such boys as these. Boys of this age it was who stood all the hard marches, who fell at Gettysburg, who endured at Andersonville, and who, when rebels said to them: 'Just pledge yourselves not to lift hand against us, but to stand by us instead, and we'll get you out of this and feed you and clothe you and fatten you up and send you home all right when you've served our cause,' answered them: 'We'll stay here and rot first!'"

Gen. Sherman said it made the tears start in his eyes at thought of all the heroism that had helped to change the boys of then into the old men of now; for he was convinced that the war had taken twenty years from a man's life!

When I reached home I had the curiosity to write to Washington and ask what had been the average age of the Army of the Potomac, and, as I have said in another place, the answer came back to me—

"Twenty-two years!"

SIGEL.

He doth nothing but talk of his horse; and he makes it a great appropriation to his own good parts that he can shoe him himself.—Merchant of Venice, Act I., Scene 2.

> Stand still, my steed—
> Let me review the scene,
> And summon from the shadowy past
> The forms that once have been.—Longfellow.

COLONEL NAGELEY of the —— regiment of —— cavalry had a remarkable horse whose name was Sigel. He came by him in a singular way. The horse belonged to Maj. Post at first, and he had trained him to throw anyone but himself. Even his grooms dared not mount him. He was a Kentucky-Whip, a bright bay gelding with massive mane and tail and the largest foretop I ever saw on a horse. His brow was very broad, with a white star in the center of it. He was about fifteen hands high, with small ears, large eyes, dilating nostrils, high, thin withers, a full chest, long shoulders and quarters and a perfect barrel. Oh, he was a beauty!

The officers' horses were all loose in corral one day, and the men were gathered about on the corral fence while the colonel was giving to his officers a lecture on the horse and his management, with a description of the differences in the methods of Rarey and Fancher. You know what a perfect horseman he was and how lithe and active; why, he could put his hand on a horse's back and hop over him. He said:

"I'd like to give you an illustration of what I am saying, if Maj. Post will trust Sigel with me for a few minutes."

"I'd trust Sigel with you, sir," said the major, "but I'd hate to trust you or any other man with Sigel."

The horse had been playing about them, and now the colonel called him to him, caressed his head and ears, and finally worked his hand down his neck and shoulders till he had it on his back, and before the horse knew what he was at, he was on him, without saddle or bridle. Sigel was frantic. He shook himself and bucked and tried every means for dismounting the colonel, who sat on him as though he was part of him. Finally, with a magnificent action, the horse dashed off on a run and leaping into the air, came down hard on his fore feet, then stopped, and filling his lungs with air, snorted it out and stood still, trembling and conquered. The colonel leaped from his back, and kissed him, and walked back to the officers, while Sigel followed close behind him. A shout from

162   CAMP FIRE STORIES.

the men testified to their appreciation of the colonel's feat.

Fourth of July came on Sunday that year, and the colonel ordered a chaplain's service, and that all the officers who attended be in full uniform. A pulpit was

The Colonel sat on him as though he was part of him.

improvised in front of the regimental headquarters, and the men were being marched out, when Maj. Post came into the colonel's tent in an undress.

"I ordered the officers to appear in full dress, Major," said the colonel.

Saying nothing, the major dashed out of the rear of the tent, jumped upon a horse and galloped away. Just then, instead of the chaplain, the senior major mounted the platform and began a speech to the colonel, telling him of the affection for him of his men, and in their behalf presented him, from the private soldiers of his command, the beautiful horse Sigel, that was just then led out all saddled and bridled. He said that the men had clubbed their resources and bought this superb animal of the major, who would have parted with him for no one else.

The colonel, taken wholly by surprise, made a response as best he might, accepting the noble gift, which was the more valued as it represented the affection of his twelve hundred men, and was to be before his eyes in the form of the most perfect horse in Tennessee.

Sigel became as much attached to the colonel as he had been to the major, though he did not seem to lose his affection for his former master; and he was perfectly docile under the colonel's saddle. Fleet as he was, he yet carried a seat like a cradle, and many a charming ride did the colonel enjoy, both during the war and for long afterwards in his northern home, where Sigel became the pet of the family and would carry the colonel's little sons upon his back with the quietness of a cart-horse.

He was intelligent, too, and the colonel used to say that he knew more than some voters. He would not only play tag with the men on the parade ground, for he was let roam at will as a house-dog would be, but he showed signs of thought.

Every day he would come into the colonel's tent and search for an apple that his master would hide. One day the colonel had an attack of ague, followed by

He began to lick the hot hand.

a high fever, and was lying on his cot when Sigel came in. The horse poked about with his nose through the tent and sniffed at the colonel's pockets till he chanced to touch his hand. All at once his ears dropped and he began to lick the hot hand and then went out of the tent. The colonel called for a servant to bring him some water, and as no one responded, again and again he called, and though he could hear voices outside, his call was not answered.

Thoroughly provoked, he managed to get to his tent-pole and push up the flap, and found that Sigel was just outside standing guard over him. Any one who attempted to enter the tent he would attack with open mouth. As soon as he saw the colonel on his feet again he gave every demonstration of joy. The colonel used to tell of this and say that, while it was a sort of "back-hand" intelligence, yet it showed that Sigel thought.

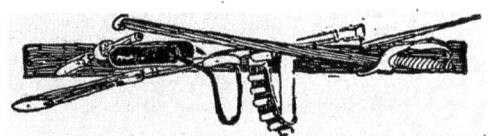

SIGEL II.

> Anger is like
> A full-hot horse, who being allowed his way,
> Self-mettle tires him. —Henry VIII, Act I, Sc. 1.

> Broad are these streams—my steed obeys,
>   Plunges and bears me through the tide.
> Wide are these woods—I thread the maze
>   Of giant stems, nor ask a guide.
> I hunt till day's last glimmer dies
>   O'er woody vale and grassy height;
> And kind the voice, and glad the eyes
>   That welcome my return at night. —Bryant.

> Roushan's tasseled cap of red
> Trembled not upon his head,
>   Careless sat he and upright;
> Neither hand nor bridle shook,
> Nor his head he turned to look,
>   As he galloped out of sight.—Longfellow.

SAID that Colonel Nageley was sure Sigel knew more than some voters, and surely he was singularly intelligent; though I am convinced that a horse — or, for that matter, any animal—who is made a pet, and so is brought into close and constant contact with a person, seems to partake of that person's ways and manner of thinking. Bright as Sigel was at the front, he seemed to develop yet more of what seemed to be intellect when he was brought North and became a member of the Colonel's family.

The children loved him and played about him, while he seemed not only to be careful about harming them, but I am convinced he would have been a protector if any one had attempted to interfere with them. Every one in town, and most people in the county, knew Sigel; and it seemed as if a whole village would turn out to see him when the Colonel rode through it on him—for Sigel never was disgraced by having on a harness.

Two stories the Colonel loves to tell about that remarkable horse.

One day having occasion to ride into the country on an errand, he took a swift gallop on Sigel, and being in something of a hurry, he ran into the farm-house, leaving the horse unhitched, as usual, at the gate. On coming out and going to the horse to mount him for his return, Sigel, in a sportive way, backed just enough to prevent his taking the bridle-rein. He kept backing away from the Colonel without looking behind him, his eyes being kept on his master and friend, and ran against a cow that was lying down. She sprang to her feet, and then all the fun in the horse broke loose and he ran about snorting and kicking up his heels. The Colonel was provoked, and said, as he sat down on a stump by the road-side:

"Take your time! When you are ready to stop your capers, come to me, for I'm in a hurry."

As soon as he so sat down Sigel came trotting right up to him. The angry Colonel sprang into the saddle and, for the first and only time, struck him sharply with his riding whip, which he had heretofore carried only for the form of the thing. The astonished horse, with almost a shriek, dashed off across the country,— over ditches, fences, fields,—in a frantic race, as though beside himself; and the Colonel let him go. When at last he stopped, as if surprised at himself as well as at this new showing of his rider, the now repentant Colonel jumped off, and said:

"Old boy, you are right and I'm wrong. I ought to have known better. I'll punish myself by walking. You may scamper round as you please. I'm awfully sorry."

Sigel ran up to him as he started to walk and put his nose on his shoulder as if in token of reconciliation. The Colonel took his head between his hands in a caress and kissed him. He said he was sure tears were in the beautiful eyes of the noble horse, as they certainly were in his own, and peace was declared. He never carried a whip after that.

At one time the Colonel rode down town, and when against the public park, which had about it a low rail fence, he met his family physician and stopped to speak to him, still sitting on his horse. On the opposite side of the park lived Guido Caracci, his regimental chief bugler, who, now the war was over and he had no more the fear of army discipline, determined to have a joke on his former commanding officer. So coming out with his bugle he sounded "Right about." Sigel whirled round, as the Colonel said, so as to make his legs stand out like the arms of the governor of an engine, when the bugler sounded "Charge." Across the road, over the fence and across the park dashed the cavalry horse, while the bugler laughed so that he could not sound the "Halt." Just as he put up his bugle to bring Sigel to a stand, the horse leaped the second fence and ran his nose into the very mouth of the bugle, upsetting the bugler and loosening his front teeth. The Colonel always insisted upon it that Sigel laughed.

The town where Colonel Nageley lived is full of stories of the remarkable sagacity which this noble horse displayed.

Major Post, who had formerly owned Sigel, and from whom the privates of the regiment bought him for a present to the Colonel, was the one described in my story of "The Devoted Major," and who was shot in saving the life of his Colonel. He was now helpless as to his lower limbs, and was obliged to be trundled about by his man in a rolling-chair. He was wealthy and had a large house, with a lawn sweeping down from the back of his mansion to the river. One day the Colonel received from him the following letter:

"My Dear Colonel—I don't expect to be long for th's world—though with my six-foot-two I have always been considered so—and I still hold my old love for Sigel, who never would have gone to any one but you. I wish, now the war is over, you'd let me have him, as a loan, while I live; and I pledge him to be returned to you when I die. I have the means for making him happy, and surely you don't need to be told that I will do so. I'm sort of lonely and want such a companion, for my dogs have no such associations in my mind. If you can' do without him for a while, and will ride one of your other horses,—content to come and see him, and me, once in a while,—you will make me very happy.

"Your old   MAJOR."

That the grateful Colonel rode Sigel over to the Major, and turned him over to that gentleman, goes without saying.

The Major had a rustic seat built on his rear lawn, and when he was placed on it, the horse was turned loose to caper about him. The man would cut grass and put it on the Major's lap, and Sigel would stand by to be fed by his hand. He seemed to realize the change in his old master, and was as tender as a kitten with him, seeming to strive for ways of amusing him.

The Colonel says that on his first visit to the Major, some time after he had taken over the horse, as he was sitting with his old friend in the rustic seat on the lawn, Sigel, who had shown every delight when he came, took his coat between his teeth and pulled him, then went off a little way and came back to do it again.

"He wants you to go with him," said the Major. "Go, and see what he is after."

The horse led the Colonel to the stable, and directly to where his bridle and saddle hung on the outside of his box-stall, poking them with his nose.

"Guy! he wants a scamper," cried the Colonel. "John, saddle the dear old fellow, and we'll take a rollic."

There was a delighted horse—and man—when once again they were together for a race across the country. Who cared for roads, when there were fences and fields? The Colonel talked to Sigel, and Sigel whinnied back; and when they returned, and the Colonel was by the Major once more, and the horse had been rubbed down and was again on the lawn,—after the Colonel had described the glorious motion and the cradle-like gait of the superb "Kentucky whip,"—as the Major, with a sigh, said in a plaintive voice, "I'd like to take a good ride on the dear old fellow," the beautiful horse put his nose into the Major's hand and licked it, as though he understood, and was sorry, too.

The Colonel had at one time entertained at his house some sweet Norse singers from Bergen; and when they came back to his town and were once again his guests, they told him that when in the Major's town they had seen a gentleman being pushed in a wheel-chair by his attendant, and there was running along in the street the most beautiful horse they had ever seen. They stopped to look at him, when he came running up to them, somewhat to their alarm.

"Don't fear him," said the gentleman. "He is a pet of mine and goes with me as a dog would. He's gentle and kind, and I don't wonder that you attract him—the more if he could have heard you sing, as I did last night."

They asked him if there was a history that belonged to the beautiful creature; and when he told them it was Colonel Nageley's horse and had formerly been his, and they assured him that they knew the Colonel very well, he sent for their baggage at the hotel and made them his guests while they stayed there. But he wouldn't tell them much of the story, only of the kindness of the Colonel in letting him have his old pet.

Then the Colonel, with a thrill in his voice, gave them the history of the horse and of the Major's glorious self-sacrifice, which they heard with tears.

The Major still lives, helpless as ever; and he kept Sigel—for the Colonel never would take him back, though he often went to see him and have a grand ride on him. But, except for the Colonel, he was never saddled, and certainly never was harnessed, though the Colonel often urged the Major to ride after him and get some good out of him in that way.

The bright, sweet-tempered horse died when he was twenty-four years old—in a serene horse-old-age—and a simple slab on the Major's lawn, close by the rustic-seat, bears the single word:

"Sigel."

COLONEL NAGELEY'S BREVET.

There was mounting in hot haste the steed,
The muttering squadron, and the clattering car,
Went pouring forward with impetuous speed,
And swiftly forming in the ranks of war;
And near, the beat of the alarming drum
Roused up the soldier, ere the morning star;
While thronged the citizens with terror dumb,
Or whispering, with white lips—the foe! they come, they
    come!   —Byron, Childe Harold, III, 25.

He proved the best man i' the field; and for his meed was brow-crowned with the oak.—Cariolanus, Act. II, Sc. 2.

COLONEL NAGELEY told me the story as I sat by his cot in the tent, where he was still laid by with his hurts. He was ordered out for a reconnoissance, with his full brigade of cavalry, with instructions not to bring on an engagement unless it was unavoidable; though I have an idea that the old Division Commander would have been surprised if a dashing cavalryman like the Colonel would come back without one. He had his own brigade of some four thousand men, a section of sixteen-pound Napoleons and a battery of Jackass guns (mountain-howitzers). Three young officers of other commands had gained permission to accompany him as aids, for the purpose of instruction; one of whom—a Major Grout—was of the engineer corps, and an experienced artillery soldier.

The morning was raw and damp, so that the men found their hands numb as they held their bridles, and it was yet dark as the column marched out of the entrenchments. Attached to the command were a hundred wagons to be filled with forage that was needed for the whole command. It was a comfortless day that was promised, both as to weather, the country to be traversed and the duty to be performed.

It was barely eight when the videttes fell back, announcing a force as large as his own, and scouts came in with an estimate of the force to be met, which led the Colonel to prepare for a pretty stiff engagement.

I don't propose to go into a description of the all-day-long battle that ensued, as it has been repeatedly given in the histories of our war. What I am at is to give the stories of individual experiences:—of all the flankings, the enfilade firings, the artillery duels, the dismounting men with every fourth man left with the horses, and all that, one can read in any story of a cavalry fight.

The Colonel had been wounded in both legs in an early battle in the war, and the holes which the Johnnies had made were closed up and healed; and though he was a little lame, yet it did not affect his magnificent horsemanship, of which I have spoken in the first story of "Sigel."

He had gone to see about a regiment that had been placed to cover one of the flanks, when an unexpected fire of artillery was opened on his centre; and, fearing that the enemy might take advantage of its effect to break his line, he was riding at full speed to rally the men there, when, as he was leaping his horse over a fence, a bullet struck the noble animal (not Sigel, for he never took him into a fight), and he came down in a heap, rolling over the Colonel, bursting open the old wounds in his legs, and, as he said, making him feel thin as paper, and all numb with prickles all over him. The boys pulled the dead horse off, and got their officer on his feet, expecting to find him helpless. But he called for another horse, half emptied a canteen of—buttermilk—that one of the fellows handed him, and was put upon the new charger.

He rallied the men, silenced the battery that had done the mischief, and drove the enemy a half mile further back. But the country was evidently made with a view to just such a battle, for it was all cut up into rifts of the rock that served for rifle-pits; and the fight lasted all the morning, as he held the enemy while his wagons were filled from fields of standing corn and large bins of it that had already been stored by the planters.

While he was holding them so at bay, the Colonel was helped upon a rock, and with his field-glasses saw the General who commanded the "Confeds" surrounded by his staff upon an eminence a half mile or so away. He called for Major Grout and asked him to sight a couple of the Napoleons—one to dismount a gun that was harrying him, and the other to drop a shell into the midst of the group of officers.

Bang! Bang! went the guns, under the practised eye of the young engineer, and the enemy's gun was knocked off its trunnions, while the General's staff was knocked hors de combat and the General was down! But he was up again, with only a dead horse to answer for the one the Colonel had lost in the early morning.

While he was rejoicing over this manoeuvre and was complimenting the Major on his correct eye, a round shot struck the rock on which he was standing and shivered it, throwing him upon the ground, bruised from fragments of stone, but yet so numb from his morning's experience that he could not tell how badly he was hurt. The Major and men rushed to him and lifted him up. He found no bones were broken, and that, though he couldn't walk yet, and his boots seemed full of blood from his reopened wounds, he could still use his mind. He was helped back on his horse.

The wagons were gathered and the retreat was sounded, when it was found that the enemy were working round his flanks, and the fight had to be all over again—in both retreat and advance.

Just as it was coming toward night, and when he had fought his way back to within a couple of miles of the entrenchments, his ordnance officer reported to him that the ammunition for the Napoleons was gone, and the men had but little left for their carbines! There was yet some for the Jackass guns.

"Shell the woods with the howitzers," said he, "and make as much noise with them as you can. If we must charge, we have our sabres yet!"

All at once he heard firing on his front, and the enemy was falling off on his flanks. What did it mean? Was a fresh reinforcement opening fire on his men who were on the flanks? Ah, ha! It was soon made clear. A young officer rode up to him and asked:

"Is this Colonel Nageley?"

"Yes; what is it?"

"Colonel Dick Mather's compliments; and he requests that you will draw in your troops about the wagons, and he will take up this little fight and relieve your men."

"What has he there?"

"A full brigade of infantry and forty rounds to the man."

The Colonel gave the necessary orders, and as his troops were coming in, he told some of the boys to lift him off his horse and lay him on the grass; and, said he:

"I tell you, I was that weak and tired and sore, and the relief was so great, that I turned over with my face down in the grass, and blubbered like a baby. I did the rest of my trip into the fortress in an ambulance, and here I've been ever since."

It was many weeks before the Colonel was able for duty again, and he didn't get the holes in his legs closed up for months; but when he did return to his command it was with a brevet for that day's work, and now he is General Nageley.

BUMMERS.

Give them great meals of beef, and iron and steel, they will eat like wolves, and fight like devils.—Henry V., Act III., Scene 7.

> The gates of mercy shall be all shut up,
> And the flush'd soldier, rough and hard of heart,
> In liberty of bloody hand, shall range
> With conscience wide as hell.
> Henry V., Act III., Scene 3.

THE BUMMER was *sui generis*. Cool, impudent, daring, he would go through a house, and cellar if it had one, a "spring-house," barn and poultry-yard, with a perfect nonchalance, and a keenness of search that nothing could evade. Burying things in the earth did no good, for he was sure to find them with his prodding. As he came into camp he was a picture; his own body and that of his horse being covered with all manner of useful and useless things, animate and inanimate, that he had captured. Chickens, ducks, geese, sucking pigs, cans of milk, butter, cheese, vegetables, tinware and sometimes

The bummer's return to camp.

blankets and even linen; anything that could be was "pressed." At one time in Southwest Mississippi a lot of them came into camp, each one of them riding in some conveyance to which he could fasten his horse: coaches, carryalls, rockaways, old buggies, wagons, tip-carts, and even a sulky. A two-horse family barouche would have the horse of the soldier fastened to one side of the pole. It was a motley crowd and every plantation for miles about had been robbed of its family carriage. Most of them were old and dilapidated and many of them useless. But they were loaded with "truck."

Most of the farmers, particularly in Tennessee, made their own whisky, each one having a little copper still, but it seemed of no avail for them to bury their product, as they often did. A bummer seemed able to smell out a keg of whisky at any depth, and a sabre or bayonet sunk in the earth would reveal it. Next to whisky, seemed to be a passion for milk to put into their coffee.

"Them caows like it," said one of them; "they jest 'lot on't. You'd orter see one of 'em, a reposin' her horns in the hands of a couple of fellers in a fence corner, and her tail just layin' in another, while one on us was on either side of her a milkin' into our tin cups and she jist a squirmin' with satisfaction. An' when we had got through with her, you'd jest orter see her a sailin' away, fairly singin' with the good time she'd had, and a longin' to tell the rest on 'em how nice it was. Oh, they enjoy it, they do."

All of this bumming was of course out of order

and was forbidden. But it was strange that officers so seldom heard or saw! Sometimes it seemed to be necessary, even aside from our living off the country for our own supply and the "war-measure." Men living on bacon and hard-tack in a hot climate were in danger of scurvy, and fresh provisions were of the first moment. Of course the proper way was for the commissary to gather all this up, and give a voucher "to be paid on proof of loyalty," but the bumming instinct was outside of that.

Yet how good and refreshing when a man was hot and his throat was choked with dust, was a good, deep drink of buttermilk! And after we had been living for a long time on our rations, how like a wisp of home air would taste a "chowan" (I don't know its orthography, but it means a spring onion) fresh from the ground, and that would send a tingle to our very extremities as it started a new life in our stagnating blood. They seemed to revitalize one so completely that gratitude made us realize the couplet in the Induction to the "Taming of the Shrew."

> "To rain a shower of commanded tears,
> An onion will do well for such a shift."

But bummers were often useful as scouts for penetrating all parts of the country, and with their eyes open, they could learn about the enemy and his movements. They were frequently in danger of capture, but they became very adroit, and though they always were ready enough to take chances, they were seldom

BUMMERS. 183

caught. Who can forbear a smile at the pictures that have been made of "Sherman's bummers" during that march to the sea when bumming was made a legitimate part of war?

When bumming was made a legitimate part of war.

CAPT. PHIL RITCHIE'S RIDE.

Courage in danger is half the battle.—Plautus.

By how much unexpected, by so much
We must awake endeavor for defense:
For courage mounteth with occasion.
—King John, Act II., Scene 1.

HIL. RITCHIE was captain of Company —, in the —— —— regiment of —— cavalry, and was one of the coolest fellows that ever wore the blue and sported the double bars in his shoulder-straps. At one time, while on staff duty, he went to carry dispatches to the general commanding division, and on his return thought he would take a short-cut through the woods and by a cart-path that he had often traversed. But it had been snowing just enough to cover his usual points of guidance, and he soon became aware that he was off his path and was lost! The night was without a moon, and only the white snow kept it from being very dark. While he was

186   CAMP FIRE STORIES.

roaming about, hoping that his horse might bring him out to the little village which he knew he should reach, if he followed the right way, he saw a glimmer of light, and rode up to it. It came from a little log-house, and a road seemed to lie beyond it.

Captain Phil Ritchie's ride.

He knocked on the door with his pistol-stock, and as it flew open he discovered that the house was filled with guerillas. As coolly as though he was at his own camp-fire, he said:

"Will you tell me which way lies the village of Cartersville?"

"H'm! yes," said one of them. "You just keep on down that thar road to yer right, and it'll fetch ye out."

"Thank you," said the captain, as he raised to his lips a whistle he had and sounded "to the right," "only this I have to say, I've got you spotted, and if you have told me wrong, I'll hang every mother's son of you."

"Lord! have you got a troop with ye?" asked one of them. The captain laughed, and said:

"Are officers apt to be riding round here in the night alone and in full uniform?"

"Say, Bill," said the last speaker of them, "ye bain't right; what's got ye? Cartersville is jest a bit round there to the left."

"All right," said the captain, as with his whistle he sounded the counter-order, "I'll soon know," and turning, he shouted, "A half dozen of you watch here till I see to the command!"

Then he walked his horse round into the road, and when he was beyond where they would hear, he told me he "just picked that horse up between his spurs and—got."

He had a hard ride of it, till he came within a couple of miles of camp and to a place where two roads crossed, and once again in thick woods, and saw, down the road to the right some fires that were burning, and, supposing that the men were choppers of his own company who had been detailed on the "wood-squad,"

"I've got you spotted."

and who often stayed out over night, he rode down to them, only to discover that he had surprised a reconnoitering squad of guerillas.

One of them sprang to his gun that was leaning against a stump, and the captain, quick as thought, said:

Guerillas reconnoitering.

"Yes, fire! It will do as well in bringing them up," and putting his shrill whistle to his lips he sounded, "Forward, gallop!" Meantime turning his horse and riding back to the road as though to hasten his men, waking the echoes of the night with his whistle.

But the bushwhackers were running, too, in the opposite direction and into the thick woods. The captain made a short ride into camp, and hastily calling and mounting a squad, rode swiftly back to the cross roads and captured the guns that the terrified Johnnies had left. When he told me of it he said:

"I reckon those chaps are running yet!"

CANNON-BALLS.

The nimble gunner,
With lynstock now the devilish cannon touches,
And down goes all before him.
                    —Henry V., Act III. Chorus.

Like feather bed betwixt a wall
And heavy brunt of cannon-ball.—Hudibras.

WHEN I was a little boy my grandfather used to take me on his knee and tell me stories of the war of 1812, when, I think, he commanded a letter-of-marque in the service of the United States —a war that was no more remote from then than our war of the rebellion is from now. I remember that, among other things, he told me of a time when he chanced to be ashore on Long Island, as the British ships of war were firing at some force of ours that had landed—I can't remember back fifty years to call up all the details of his story—and he saw a twelve-pound shot slowly rolling along the beach; he put out his foot to stop it and it took off the heel of his boot and rolled on unimpeded. He thought it was lucky that it hadn't taken off his leg, as it would have done as easily if he hadn't happened to tackle it as he did. He said to me, I remember:

"Never try to stop a cannon-ball." Well, I never did try to.

I used to think as I remembered that story of my grandfather's that he might have been "drawing the long bow," till I had seen a round shot rolling on the ground that one would think might be easily stopped, but that would take off a sapling and not have its progress very materially checked.

Balls played strange freaks afield sometimes, and they were ugly things to listen to as they crashed through the trees above us and tore off big branches to come down on our devoted heads, even if it weren't as bad as the rotten shells that soared aloft with the "whirr-a-whirr-a-whirr-a" that every soldier so well remembers and that often rose to a very shriek as though it were some valkerie that was sweeping along above us and sounding her call for us to cross the Asa-bridge and attend the council of the gods; those shells that were liable to break up at any time and shower their death-dealing wreckage among us.

At the time I was speaking of in the story of Little Wes and his supposed bravery, my quartermaster was dismounted and standing near me, with a tree in range (why should I allow him to endanger his precious life when it would do no good, and a quartermaster was of vital importance to a command), and his bridle-rein was slipped over his arm. He was a lame man, with one leg shorter than the other, but as agile as a cat, and a capital soldier as well as accountant, and at this time was A. Q. M. G., and on my staff, for I was commanding brigade.

A shell explodes.

He would joke about his infirmity, and laugh at having his stirrups of unequal length, and all that, and when I warned him not to attempt to stop an innocently rolling six-pound round-shot, that afterward went through a half-rotted stump and kept on its way, he said, in his jocular way:

"I'd a had to shorten more or even up my stirrups if I'd tried to stop it—according to which leg I'd put out!"

While he was standing there I saw a twelve-pounder rolling toward a tree near him, and shouted to him to look out that it didn't make a carom on him, and, sure enough, it struck a big elm, and started across at an angle toward him. He took a "dot-and-go-one" jump to the side of the tree, when the ball hit another tree and took a fresh angle as though starting for him again. He dropped his bridle-rein and let his horse run away, while he hopped round the tree to get behind the ball, shouting:

"Lord! I'm elected!"

But he came out all right and his horse was caught, so that no harm came of it.

IMPRESSIVE SERVICES.

> Ah, why
> Should we in the world's riper years, neglect
> God's ancient sanctuaries, and adore
> Only among the crowd, and under roofs
> That our frail hands have raised?—Bryant.

The Most High dwelleth not in temples made with hands.
—Acts 7: 48.

CHAPLAIN service was often held as early as five o'clock in the morning on account of the heat. It was always interesting and instructive, and especially when we could listen to men like McCabe or Chidlaw. The parade ground was nicely policed the night before, and the men were all dressed in their best, as though for the ten-o'clock inspection, while the officers attended in full uniform. Then the band led in the singing and the prayers would waken tender memories of home as the chaplain besought a blessing on the dear absent ones. Rough men were softened, and a holier influence pervaded the day. Usually there was a Sunday school and a prayer-meeting sometime in the day, conducted by the chaplain or by some one of the soldiers who was a Christian man.

Then there was the visitation of hospital, and a kindly word spoken to poor fellows who were sick or hurt, maybe by the colonel or the company officers, with reminiscence of home, and hearty congratulations on some act of bravery on the part of the patient.

The funerals, too, were touching occasions, when the burying squad carried the body for its interment, with reversed arms and to the slow, sad tune of the "Dead March in Saul," and with the salute fired over the grave; even if we did march back to the tune of "The girl, the girl, the pretty, pretty girl, the girl I left behind me." It was not that we forgot the fellow that we had put into his far away and maybe to be unknown grave, but we were always facing death, and never knew in the morning but we might be killed before night, and it didn't do to let our minds rest too much on the solemnity of the fact. We must needs make light of death, on the principle of the old Norse idea, that only he who died with his buskins on could enter the halls of Valhalla and drink of the mead of the gods. The fellows that had died in battle were offered sacrifices on the altar of country, and we loved to think that

> "Christ hath died to make men holy,
> We must die to make men free;"

And there is glory in death that is for the saving of native-land. It meant being enshrined in the most sacred niche in the hearts of countrymen, and the realizing that we shed blood for the redemption of home and its dear ones to untold generations.

But the most sacred event of each day was at the dress-parade, when the command was drawn up in line,

The funerals were touching occasions.

with the band at the right of it, the colonel in full uniform before it, and midway between him and the regiment the adjutant, when the order came:

"First sergeants to the front and center. March!"

And they came into line together, band-master and

all. Then each one came to the salute in turn, as though he placed his hand on his beating heart and reported.

"All present, or accounted for!"

We used, sometimes, to look on to the day of the final dress-parade, when we stood before the Great Commander and each gave report of the responsibilities of life, and wonder if we could each put his hand on his heart and echo what there we heard:

"All present, or accounted for!"

JACK BOSWELL.

I was an hungered, and ye gave me no meat; I was thirsty, and ye gave me no drink.—Matt. 25: 42.

I have given you an example, that ye should do as I have done to you.—John 13: 15.

JACK BOSWELL was a lawless fellow; an ideal cavalryman on account of his reckless dash, he was so full of life and fire and haze —and too often of "Robinson County" whisky—as to be often in trouble and not infrequently in the guardhouse. He was the lightest for riding at the test of horses on the course and could take a hurdle the easiest of any, and he was the fastest sprinter, the highest jumper, and the leader in the camp-fire dance when some little nigger was set to patting. Wicked enough he was, and yet there was an ingenuousness about him that made you feel that what he did was natural and was not so wrong. "Oh, it's just Jack Boswell, and he can't help it," the boys would say.

In a stiff little brush that we had Jack was shot in both ankles and had to have a double amputation. Both his feet were taken off! Poor Jack was frantic about it.

"To think, sir," he said, "that I've got to hobble all my days and to go slow—to be a poke! What girl will look at a fellow with no feet! I can't ride any more, or have any times! Oh, I wish it had taken off the other end of me. I'd rather be shorter a head! I'd rather be dead!"

Poor Jack was in the hospital, and it was hot. There were flies buzzing about and mosquitoes sang doleful songs in a very monotonous manner. There was a combined smell of the applications made to wounds and of the antiseptics in form of chlorides then in use; and even the sweet-faced and black-robed sisters of charity who tried to alleviate the sufferings of the poor fellows and to while away the time that hung so heavily upon them, were of little avail against what was worse than even the pain, the homesickness that was not less poignant because it was given the more scientific name of "nostalgia."

Jack lay there with only a sheet over him, but feeling the clammy sweat that came partly from his pain and partly from his heat, and holding a fan that had been given to him by the sister who had been sitting by him and now was called to another suffering patient. He had studied out every figure on the paper on the wall, and had watched the convolutions of a swarm of flies that were seeming to play tag over his head, and he was thinking of a cool shade beneath an

A lady with a little basket on her arm came into the ward.

elm that stood near his home in the north and under which he had often lain and napped on hot summer days. Oh, he was fuming at thought that never again could he range the huckleberry fields or the chestnut woods, or chase the girls about the corn-pile at the husking-bees on the old home farm.

A lady with a little basket on her arm came into the ward, and Jack fixed his greedy eyes upon her. Oranges or cool bananas or fresh figs came into his mind, and a possible apple, though the apples south were not so juicy and crisp as they were out of the old home orchard. She would have something that was good, and Jack was thirstier than he had ever felt, a thirst which the luke-warm water that the blessed sister had given him didn't seem to slake. He wanted something juicy and tart.

The lady came to his bed and said:

"Ah, my poor fellow (that did Jack good), I have brought you something that I hope will help you (that did Jack more good), and I hope you'll take it and read it prayerfully."

She gave Jack a tract that she took from her little basket, and passed on to dispense her store of a like kind to other poor, thirsty, hot, suffering men.

Jack fairly groaned. The disappointment was so great! But he took up the tract, shielded his eyes with his fan and read its title: "From a Ball-room to Hell!" It was on the sin of dancing!

As the lady came back down the ward, Jack said:

"May I see you a moment, madame?"

"Certainly," she said. "I hope I have done you

good this morning. I am deeply interested in the spiritual condition of you men who may not have long to live."

"I thought so," said Jack, "and I give you my pledge that I'll never dance again. I've been a pretty tough nut in my day, but that nut's cracked now. I'm done with it all."

"God be-praised!" cried she as she rolled up her eyes.

"Pull up the sheet at the bottom of the bed," said Jack.

She did so, and her eyes dilated with horror as she saw that his feet were gone.

COURAGE IN BATTLE.

> Courage is, on all hands, considered as an essential of high character.—Froude.

> That all men would be cowards if they dare,
> Some men we know have courage to declare.—Crabbe.

>   I argue not
> Against heaven's hand or will, nor bate a jot
> Of heart or hope; but still bear up and steer
> Right onward.   —Milton.

IN MY article on "Bravery," I allude to the fact that I am often asked,—as is, I suppose, every old soldier,—"What are the sensations on going into battle?" In several of these stories I have tried to describe some of them. For a man to have no fear, I should imagine he must be either a stick or a dolt. If he is neither, and yet says he has none, I should think he was lying.

That sense of fear may be of many different kinds. It may be in dread of hurts, and the pain of them, and the long life crippled because of them; or it may come of dread of the hospital, its heat and flies and thirst; or it may be, as with a friend of mine who was an accomplished pianist and feared the loss of his fingers; or it may be a fear of the effect of his wounding or death on his loving, and perhaps dependent family; or it may be a fear of how one will act, if he can properly handle his men, and do his duty in every way; or it may be the fear of death and a dread of what will come after it:—but in all these cases it is fear, and it may not necessarily be terror.

I can see a deal of difference between the one which is dread, and the other which is consternation and panic; and which would lead a man to run away because his legs got the better of him, like the sorry victim whom Marryatt describes in "Japhet in Search of His Father."

I don't know as it is any disgrace to a man to have sensitive nerves, or a keen appreciation of the value of life or a life that is lived in a body which has not been mutilated. But where a person has this sensitive nature and yet goes into a hell of bullets and shells, it is bravery. I told the story of "Little Wes" and of his facing a battery; but that was not bravery, it was ignorance. When he came to know, he was an abject coward. What he found out made him feel as described by Hamlet's father's ghost:

"Harrow up thy soul; freeze thy young blood;
Make thy two eyes, like stars, start from their spheres;
Thy knotted and combined locks to part,
And each particular hair to stand on end,
Like quills upon the fretful porcupine."

Those "knotted and combined locks" of Wes' were simply coming out of kink, and he was turning into a white man!

But we never had a fight in which men who, when they went in, were "white about the gills" and trembling so that their knees fairly smote together, didn't go through the fight as bravely as any one, coming out heroes; but to have precisely the same experience at the next battle.

Many a public speaker has a similar sensation as he goes before an audience; but loses the fear when he begins to speak, and has no vestige of it when he is warmed up with his subject.

Really, it is not a very pleasant thing to know that you are to stand up all day as a target for a few thousand men, every one of whom wants to hit you, and to hit to kill. Would you like to do it for thirteen dollars a month, and depreciated currency at that; and with the sense that it wouldn't be many years before pretty much everybody would forget that you had done it, or knew or cared that you did? Would you do it for thirteen thousand dollars a day?

But numbers help to make a man brave—or, at least, to appear so. A fellow don't like to seem a coward to his comrades; and the fact of a brave fellow by you is a spur to you.

But, once in a battle, a new factor appears. One seems to lose every sense, and to have every nerve dulled by the condition of things that are about him and in him. There is the confusion of the awful noise; the rattle of rifles, the booming and confusion of cannon, the cries of men and horses that are hurt, the dense smoke of burning powder. There is the fearful thirst that comes upon a man, and that is known as "the powder-thirst," which comes of the air being full of the fumes of sulphur and nitre, which seem to dry up every juice in one's throat—not to say in his body. Just how this is done no one seems to know. Dunglison says of thirst, anyhow: "Physiologists differ regarding the seat of thirst; some place it in the fauces, others in the stomach. Its immediate cause is not known. It has been attributed to a dry condition of the nervous papillæ of the pharynx, produced by suppression of the salivary and mucous secretions. This is probably true. Thirst is an internal sensation, an instinctive want arising from organization, and inexplicable." But the fact is very tangible.

If the explosion of powder in cannon makes the heavens weep in showers, it dries up the tears in the soldier. One can seem to hear his tongue rattle against his teeth. There is, added to this, the dreadful sense of fatigue that one never appears to feel at any time so much, and which comes of all these elements combined, added to the exertion he puts forth.

In visiting foreign cities and roaming through cathedrals, and galleries of art, and palaces, and the like, one does more than he thinks he does; and when the day is over he sinks down in utter exhaustion. It is exaggerated in a battle, but the fatigue is realized pretty soon.

This seems to attack even one's sensibilities, dulling his nerves so that he not only forgets fear, but even his affections become blunted. I remember, one day, when the regiments of my command were placed in different positions on the field, an aid came to me and I was giving him an order to the Colonel of one of the regiments. I was looking off on the field and watching a movement of some troops as he was asking me more definitely about the order I had given him, when he stopped in the middle of his question. I looked round at him just in time to see that he was falling from his horse and to catch him. He was shot through the head. I called a couple of men to take him and lay him on the ground; and I remember even during that I did not care, any more than if the ball had struck a tree. Yet that man was my dearest friend in the army, a fellow-townsman, and my tent-mate! After the battle was over, when I was rested and had become normal, I mourned for him bitterly; and grieved with the beautiful young wife who had been made a widow so early, and for the two sweet little girls that were fatherless.

One can't have the emotion of fear at such a time and under such thrilling circumstances, any more than he can have any other emotion. I have tried to show this in my story of "The Sharp-Shooters." It is simply a matter of indifference to everything.

Of course, over and above all this is principle. A patriot has gone into the army for a great cause that is dearer to him than his life; and when he comes to realize what depends on him, both in saving his men and his country, it overpowers and overtops every feeling besides. This I tried to show in my chapter on "Bravery," in the case of the Captain of Co. A of the ——— Regiment of ——— Cavalry. Under such a sense one could hardly help being brave.

Yet I am thinking of those noble women at home, who had no spur to their patriotism, but who let husband or son or father go into the army; and then must sit down and think and suffer and dread the gazettes. I'm not sure but this was a large factor with a good many men, who felt that big eyes were on them, full of tears; and yet with a flush of pride on the cheeks, at thought that they were sharing the heroism of men who were dying for country.

However, it is a hard thing to analyze.

THE HOSPITAL HYMN.

Thy pathway lies among the stars.—Longfellow.

A single star
Sparkles new—set in heaven.—Bryant.

Our echoes roll from soul to soul,
And grow forever and forever.—Tennyson.

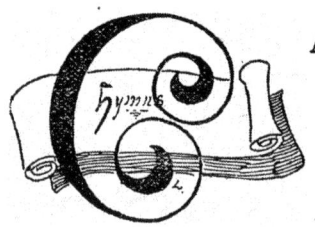

CAN ANYONE imagine anything hotter, sultrier, more provoking of fever than an Alabama hospital in August, when all the atmosphere seems to be dried up and changed to a viewless but realized dust, like that in the streets, and the perspiring stewards stand about, in hearing of the fever-parched patients, and crack lazy, sleepy jokes about eggs cooked by being dropped on flagged sidewalks that are red-hot? What old soldier that has ever tossed—if he could even get the relief of tossing—on those cot-beds does not remember the beginning of gangrene, and the smell of pus, and the fear of blood-poisoning, all of which seemed to breed swarms of flies by day and bigger swarms of mosquitoes at night, which to the half-dreaming, half-delirious sufferer from fever sounded like the tea-kettle of the home kitchen, but which stung and itched like the nettles and ivy of the sweltering hay-fields on the home farm and yet which bred, in turn, worse homesickness.

Who can wonder that, under all these aggravations of the pain of wounds, of knitting bones that have been shattered, of awful thirst and with no ice to cool the luke-warm, insipid water, and the weakening effect of fever, strong men, who had been heroes in a fight and who had borne with never a complaint the hardships of bivouac and the fatigue of marches, should become peevish almost to the point of childishness?

They did become so, and often a man, who had been strong and stern enough in his health, would seem to be a boy again, and sometimes would cover his face with his hands and sob like a child as he lay helpless in hospital, longing for woman's hand and voice in place of the rough but kind soldier-nurses.

Charlie Bissell, who was first sergeant in Company A, and who had done heroic service in the fight till he was shot down with a bullet through his abdomen, lay on a cot by the middle window of Ward C, where he could look out and see the North Star at night, and he could always see it, for never a cloud came to obscure the heavens, as a shield to the scorching sun by day, or to send cooling showers by night. He was growing weaker every day, and paler, and thinner, and his voice had taken on a plaintiveness that was in striking contrast to the ring of it that we knew so well.

"Ah, sir," he said to the colonel one day, "mother

told me that the North Star never moved; that it was fixed as God is, and that when I looked up at it I would be looking where she looked. She said we could both of us make it a window to send prayers up to, and they'd meet there to go side by side up through to God. Mother told me that if ever I got hurt, I'd remember what she had said, but I didn't believe it would be all as plain as it is."

He lay and thought a few minutes, and then he said, while his eyes seemed to grow deeper:

"If I could only get a sniff of the air that comes down through the orchard up back of our home! You remember the old orchard up there, how large the trees are, and the apples—the Golden Sweets and the Baldwins and Greenings and Russets, and—there's a spring at the—upper end of the orchard, close—by the great rock—the Donner-rock we—always called it. Ah—mother, mother! the cup—the cup—why won't you —let me—have it? I'm so dry—I'm so—"

Charlie's voice sank into moans, lower and lower. Then he went to receive a golden chalice in place of the tin cup he had called for, and to answer a call to drink of better, cooler water from the river of the water of life, where the hot sun never shines so fearfully.

Poor Tom Tripp, who had been brought in that day, lay not far away from Charlie's cot, and he had been listening to what his first sergeant had said, while the cold sweat started out all over him, hot as the day was; and his eyes fairly stood out as the colonel put his hand on Charlie's eyelids to close them—those eyes that had been so fearless on the battle-field, so true in their love

THE HOSPITAL HYMN.   213

for a comrade, and that did not fill with terror even at the thought of death.

"Is the sergeant dead, sir?" asked Tom with a shiver.

"Yes, he's gone to the better home, Tom," said the

Charlie's voice sank into moans lower and lower.

colonel. "He was a good soldier, and he was a good Christian, Tom."

Tom turned away with a groan that sounded like an oath. He was shot in such a way that the surgeon said he might get up if it were not so hot and close; but there was little hope as it was. He was a daring, dashing fellow, a good cavalryman, with a supple wrist, but apt to be profane and intemperate. Now he was in mortal terror.

All at once came the voice of Billy Eager, he that was so loved all through the command, and whose left leg was out on the pile near the haystack under whose shade was the operating field-table—he whose eye was like an eagle's, and who was not ashamed to pray in his tent where the fellows heard him. Billy said, "Tom, you didn't come in soon enough to get Charlie's hymn."

Then he repeated a verse of it, with a voice as soft and sweet and gentle as if it belonged to some loving woman, and very different from the voice that had helped yell in the cavalry charge in which he was hurt.

> "Just as I am without one plea
> But that thy blood was shed for me,
> And that thou bidst me come to thee,
> O Lamb of God, I come."

Tom listened to the last line, and then he said, "Shut up, Bill." Then he almost shouted, "Shut up, I tell ye!" as though he heard the echo of Bill's voice yet.

Tom turned over to the wall, and gave a groan. After a little he turned his head, and there seemed to be tears in his eyes; but there was a sort of bravado in his voice as he said, "It's a lie, Bill, and you know it."

"Ah, Tom," said Billy, "I know it ain't."

"'Tis too, Bill, for such a chap as me. Say it ag'in!"

THE HOSPITAL HYMN.

Then Billy said it once more; and as though it brought an agony to his soul Tom turned to the wall again, and cried out, "Shut up! I tell ye, shut up!"

Then Billy went on—

> "Just as I am, and waiting not
> To rid my soul of one dark blot,
> To thee whose blood can cleanse each spot,
>   O Lamb of God, I come."

"Hey, what's that, Billy?" cried Tom, half raising himself in his cot, "what's that about not waitin' till—oh, bother!—say it ag'in;" and he turned his head a little to listen, while great beads of sweat stood on his flushed face.

Billy said it again very slowly; and when he was done, Tom said huskily, as though his throat was full: "Billy, do you believe it will come down to me? Say, Billy, honor bright, now. You know me. Say—I'll believe what you say. Say something you don't get from anybody else. Tell me yourself. Hey?"

"Yes," said Billy. Then he told Tom of the thief on the cross, and of the woman taken in adultery, and of Peter and his denial. Tom listened as though his life depended on Billy's words—as no doubt it did—and then he said: "Say, Billy, show me how. I'm a poor good-for-nothin', anyhow, and I may as well own up."

So Billy led the poor wounded soldier to "the Lamb of God, which taketh away the sin of the world," and who came to save to the uttermost.

A few days after, Tom, who was getting weaker and whiter, grew faint, and the old daring look was gone from his eyes. With a weak voice he said: "Billy, I reckon my time's a'most up; I wish I could see the sergeant's north star; but he's left a star for me. Say that thing ag'in, them two verses, will ye?"

So Billy said them, but his voice was husky; and Tom took up the words and said them over low, and as though he was really praying them, till he got on into the second verse:

> "Just as I am, and waiting not
> To rid my sold of one dark blot,

then he put his hand to his side with a paroxysm of pain, while a strange pallor came over his face, and with his breath growing short, he said:

> "To — thee whose — blood — can cleanse each — spot—
> O Lamb—O Lamb of God—I come — I —"

there was a little gurgle in his throat, and Tom was gone.

Angel bands came to sing the song of welcome; who doubts it? Billy said, "It was better than the north star to Charlie and Tom—that hymn; it was

> 'The star, the star of Bethlehem.' "

MULETEERS.

"Our armies swore terribly in Flanders," cried my Uncle Toby, "but nothing to this."—Tristram Shandy, Chap. XI.

Twelve young mules, a strong, laborious race.—Pope.

> You taught me language, and my profit on't
> Is, I know how to curse; the red plague rid you,
> For learning me your language."—Tempest, Act. I, Sc. 2.

AN ARMY muleteer is a rara avis, even though he came to be pretty common during the war. Just as now one has to stop and look at an electric-car go by, or watches out in the evening for the starting of the electric lights down a street—all at once—or even gazes in a wonder that never intermits at an express train gliding like a huge snake across the landscape; so one had to stop and look at and listen to a muleteer during the war; and especially if his team was stalled, or if a section of artillery was stopping up his way.

He had language! I have never heard it equaled, except by a mate of a Mississippi River steamboat under the old regime. You remember Mark Twain gives just a passing glimpse at a river-mate:

"WHERE 're you going with that barrel! *for'ard* with it 'fore I make you swallow it, you dash-dash-*dash-dashed* split between a tired mud-turtle and a crippled hearse-horse;" and then he says: "I wished I could talk like that." It is the wonderful fascination that holds anyone to the mysteriously perfect, in speech or act; and particularly in speech when it is a muleteer starting his long-eared team out of a slough or a road that is hub-deep in Southern mud. It is (perhaps) what Cowper calls the "mulish mouth of headstrong youth."

The movement of an army was always an exciting scene. It called vividly to mind pictures by Homer and Dante and Milton; and the shrieking mules, whose heels seemed the highest and busiest parts of them, answered for the rushing, howling spectres; and all this was helped in its hellish wildness by the cracking of the black-snake whips, the neighing of horses, the clashing of arms, the croupy cry of mules and the intense remarks of muleteers; to all which the Quartermaster gave a zest and a spice as he shouted an occasional order that might teach even the muleteer something of the variety that was prolific in the way of mixing theology with ordinary speech. Yet amid all this evident confusion—a chaos to outsiders—all would be perfect system. Not a surcingle was to be lost from a horse, nor a coat from a man, nor a side of bacon from the Commissary. The Quartermaster and Commissary had each his place and his rules for gaining that place; but the language that was involved was a matter of marvel.

A team usually was of six mules, with the driver sitting on the nigh pole mule, and guiding his team by a "jerk-rein," which led on through rings in the harness of the middle pair to the leading nigh mule, from whose bit to that of the off-leader was a slight wooden pole; so that, if the nigh mule turned to right or left, his mate felt the movement telling on his bit. The direction was given by one, or two, jerks, or a pull, on the rein, to which the mules were drilled. Then, when the "black-snake" (with which the driver could flick a fly from the ear of a leader) came into requisition, it was supplemented by an address that was ingeniously pointed.

We had, however, one muleteer who was differently made up. Jake Amey had a team of six large, gray Spanish mules, which he loved. They were always well-groomed and looked sleek and happy, even when other teams were sorry enough. Jake never swore, and seldom so much as raised his voice; and he never seemed to be stalled. Yet he would often "double-up" with other teams to help them out of some swale where they were stuck. But while he never swore nor "jawed" his mules, he was far from a man to be fooled with by the other teamsters.

One day a muleteer whom Jake was helping with his team, struck one of the pet grays of our hero; and, with an awful fist, Jake sent him sprawling to earth; and then he unhitched his team and took it back to his own wagon. He got the name among the mule-drivers of "the hard-fisted saint." But though he was a tall, powerful fellow, and struck out suddenly and fiercely from the shoulder on provocation, he was as tender as a lover with his animals.

He kept his harnesses in good condition, so that the leathers were always black and the brasses glistened in the sun; and always there were tufts of horsehair hanging in long tassels from the ears of his mules. Love them! Why, Jake slept with them, and talked to them as though they were girls. He would go without his own mess until they were fed, watched the loading of his wagon to see that it was not too heavy and that it was adjusted for the easiest carrying; and I have a suspicion that he stole ponchos to make water-proof coverings for his Spaniards in rainy weather.

Jake was not sociable with the other muleteers; though, as I said, he was always ready to use his team in helping them out; provided they didn't interfere with his method of doing it. But he would never allow any one to touch his mules.

Of course, such a man was not long unnoticed by the commanding officer; and after a while he was transferred to the Brigade Headquarters, and was given the wagon that carried all the precious matters that belonged to the Colonel commanding. Here Jake was happy, for he had little difficulty in getting forage, and his darlings were less in danger of glanders and other ills that horse-flesh is heir to.

But one day there came a calamity for poor Jake.

No sun can always shine even on the dearest affection.

In a march there was a surprise. Cannon boomed from an unexpected point and the command was quickly deployed to cover the baggage train. Many of the muleteers cut their traces and struck for the rear; but Jake stood by his mules. Firing became general and our forces seemed to be winning the day, when there came a crashing "spherical-case" right into the midst of Jake's team, and three of his mules were killed outright, while one had a leg broken, so it had to be shot. Four out of his six were dead, and his team was broken up!

Jake sat down by his dead dears like a man distracted. There were no tears; but the dazed, glassy eyes of the man showed that his affliction was too deep for that. The fight was over, and the muleteers were rallying to their wagons; and still he sat there. The Colonel said to him, in a cheery voice.

"Jake, 'there are as many good fish in the sea as ever were caught.' You shall have a team of the best mules to be found in the Department. Cheer up, old fellow; we'll stand by you."

"*They* ain't my mules," said Jake, despondently. "I've had 'em all through the war, an' I've nussed 'em an' cared fer 'em; and I knowed 'em, an' they knowed me. They're goned, an' so be I. I ain't no count no more."

Poor Jake never rallied. He became sick, and went into hospital, still the same heart-broken man—and there he died.

Talk of a man's love for animals not taking the place of every other love! Why, Jake's big Spanish mules were to him wife and children and home—they were all the world to him. Before he died he said to the Chaplain:

"Won't I find 'em, over there?"

"I reckon so," said the Chaplain.

"Good," said Jake. So he was content to die.

LITTLE PIETY.

LITTLE PIETY.

> He spake, and into every heart his words
> Carried new strength and courage.
> —Bryant's Homer's Iliad.

No act of a man, no Thing (how much less the man himself!) is extinguished when it disappears, through considerable time it still visibly works, though done and vanished.
—Carlyle.

HE COLONEL loved his men, and the men loved their colonel. I think he knew the name of every one of the twelve hundred men of his regiment, and yet I doubt if any one of them would take advantage of his being among them to indulge in any familiarity, or even breach of military etiquette; for he was a stern man on duty, and demanded every point of the army code. But if he was a martinet it was for the purpose of turning out the best cavalry regiment in the brigade. He would not let his men take off their coats in a march even though the day was hot, and of course he never marched without his own; but, then, he had the smallest sick-call of any regiment of cavalry in the command. He would appear at most unexpected times and places during stable-call, and the boys found out one day soon after he had taken command of the regiment that he meant to have everything good for them.

He strolled down by a cook who was boiling some beans for the company mess, and, looking at the kettle, he saw it was not clean, and the water looked muddy, and so did the beans, which evidently had not been picked over nor washed. The colonel was in undress uniform, and the cook did not know him.

"Are you cooking beans for the horses?" asked the colonel.

"I don't know as it's any of your business who I'm a cookin' 'em for," cried the cook with an oath.

"I asked if you were cooking them for the horses," said the colonel, with an ominous glitter to his eyes which the cook didn't like the looks of.

"No, sir, I'm cookin' on 'em for the men. I reckon they're good enough for private soldiers." The cook spoke surlily, and yet with a touch of fear, for there was something about the eyes that were fastened on him that looked powerful and ominous.

"What is your rank?" asked the colonel.

"Me? Oh, I'm a private soldier; detailed as cook."

The boys had gathered round and were listening very hopefully of something better for their mess, complaints of which had already gone to the company officers.

"Orderly, tell Capt. Jenkins to detail me a corporal and guard, immediately."

When they came the colonel said:

"I am determined that you men shall have as good

"I don't know as it's any of your business."

food and as well cooked as I have at headquarters, and you shall have it. That mess isn't fit for a pig's-trough, yet the cook says it is good enough for a private soldier, and I'm going to see if it is. Corporal, detail four of your men to hold him and feed it to him; feed him the whole of it." His voice had a vibration to it that was fearful. They were only too glad—those soldiers who had suffered from the cook's insolence and profanity, added to his nastiness—and the order was obeyed. Tears streamed from his eyes as he was obliged to swallow the hot stuff that was crammed into his mouth, and at last he managed to cry out:

"Oh, you're killing me, sir."

"I suppose so," said the colonel, very coldly.

But at last he bade them desist, merely saying as he turned on his heel:

"If I find another cook trying to foist a bad mess on any of the companies I'll have it fed to him—till he dies!"

Every week he found time to be more or less in hospital, cheering up the boys, and with a keen eye on hospital stewards and nurses; and if the chaplain ever got a specially cordial greeting from his colonel, it was when he met him in hospital busy at his sacred office with the sick and wounded soldiers.

Such was the colonel, and though he was unbending in discipline and insisted on the most rigorous drill, the keenest of inspections that involved men and horses and accoutrements, he was ready to reward those who proved themselves good soldiers, and to care for the best interests of all. Every one knew that he was fearless, not only in battle, but when it came to the enduring of hardships, for he would take them as the men did. If they had to bivouac in rain or snow, he would wrap himself in poncho and blanket and share with them the exposure.

The colonel heard the boys speak frequently of "Little Piety," and often wondered who it was that had so strange a sobriquet. At last he asked one of his orderlies:

"Who is this that you call 'Little Piety?'"

"Oh, he's a little fellow in Company L. We used to call him 'Little Piety' in a sort of a lark, sir, but we got over that long ago, for he's the real stuff. There don't nobody make no fun of him now—not much! The fellows 'd make it hot for a boy't 'd poke anything at him."

"Why, what does he do?" asked the colonel.

"Oh, he's kind of girlie like, only he ain't no girl; he's clear grit. But if any of us is sick, or in any sort of trouble—homesick like, or anything—he knows what to do or what to say that just hits the spot. Then he can choke off a fellow a swearin' and cussin', and he has got the company pretty much broke off of a-drinkin' and singin' tough songs. I don't see just how it is, but we feel meaner'n pusley if we do anything outrageous, and him looking on."

There was a man in the regiment that had been taken from the penitentiary, changing the stripes for the blue—a thing allowed short-term men in state prison. He was looked upon as a desperate character, though a good cavalryman in his way. Many were afraid of him. One day this ex-convict was swearing furiously not far from headquarters, and the colonel saw a small man come and, putting his hand on the other's arm, say to him just one word, "Don't!"

The colonel looked to see the angry man strike the brave young soldier; and if he had, there would have been guard-house duty for him; but instead, he said, while a look of genuine shame came into his face: "Beg your parding, 'Little Piety.' Didn't mean to say it. It come out afore I thought."

That was the first the colonel had seen of "Little Piety."

A man asked the colonel one day if they might have a hospital tent for Sunday.

"Why," asked the colonel, "is the chaplain going to open a Sunday school?"

"Chaplain—neau! It's 'Little Piety.'"

The colonel looked in on Sunday, and there was the little fellow surrounded by soldiers who were listening intently as he opened to them the Scriptures by telling what they were to him. He was earnest and true, and every word he spoke seemed to come out of a heart that had felt, and to fit a need among the men.

Preparations were making for a hard fight, when the colonel sent for "Little Piety," whom he had learned to know and love, and he said to him:

"I tell you frankly that you are doing a good work in the regiment, and I cannot afford to risk you. You are too small, and so is your horse, if we should have a sabre charge, as we may. I want you to take a detail and stay back with the baggage train to-morrow."

"Oh, don't keep me back, sir," cried the plucky little fellow. "I came into the service to do my duty in the field, and the men would think I was a coward if I stayed back on any excuse. Let me go, sir; do please!"

An orderly was by, who said, "Colonel, the boys will stand by 'Little Piety,' and brace him up, if he is small. They won't let him be rode over."

After the fight and the shelling of the woods, the colonel rode back over the field that had witnessed the charge of that day, and the crash of sabre to sabre and pistol and horse all breast to breast. Poor fellows lay all about, some with wide-open eyes in the glare of sunshine, as though looking after the spirit that had flown up into the brightness, and some calling for a sup from a canteen as they lay hurt and parched under the awful "powder thirst."

The colonel and his orderlies helped whom they could, and superintended the removing of the wounded. But as they came to a road over which they had charged, there was a body lying face downward in the deep dust into which blood had been soaking. Reverently the colonel turned it over, and brushed away the dust and clotted blood, only to have his worst fears realized. It was "Little Piety," with a bullet through his forehead.

The long trench was dug the next day, and in it were laid, wrapped in their blankets and placed side by side, the scores of noble men who were soon to be reckoned as "the unknown dead;" but they didn't put "Little Piety" into that long grave. Under a widespreading live oak, and where the pendent and festooned gray mosses formed cypress wreaths, there the whole regiment gathered and sung, with choking voices, the hymn he had loved so well, and which he had taught them in the hospital tent Sunday school:

> "Must Jesus bear the cross alone
> And all the world go free?
> No, there's a cross for every one,
> And there's a cross for me.
>
> "The consecrated cross I'll bear,
> Till death shall set me free,
> And then go home, my crown to wear,
> For there's a crown for me."

Strong arms were ready to help as the body was lowered in that grave, which was always to abide in the picture gallery of every soldier's mind as it was while he stood by on that day; and when the final volley was fired over the grave, strong men, who had not blanched in the face of a battery on the field, and who had endured the shock of a cavalry charge the day before, wept like children.

Years have rolled by since then, and the war has become a history, while its incidents have grown into holy memories to be told over with flashing and filling eyes by the side of camp-fires, as some old veteran

> Tells o'er his wounds or deeds of glory done,
> Shoulders his crutch, and shows how fields were won.

The old regiment was gathered in its annual reunion, and the colonel, now gray and wrinkled, had met the remnant of his grand old cavalry command at camp-fire. "Boys," said he, "there are incidents of our war that made a deeper impression on your minds than any other. I would like to have you tell which

"I thank God for Little Piety."

is most vivid." Man after man said, "'Little Piety,' sir. He started me on the right way, and I've stuck to it." At last, one man rose—tall, dignified, and showing that he was a man of means, and accustomed to position and influence in society:

"Boys," said he, "you know what I was. Some of you dared call me 'jail-bird' when I first enlisted from the penitentiary of northern ——, though"—and he gave a grim smile—"I don't remember that any one ever said it but once; but that blessed boy somehow touched me as nobody else ever did; he made me understand that Jesus came to seek and save 'the lost,' and that it meant me because I was lost. When we buried him I couldn't sing that song, but I said it down in my heart—

'The consecrated cross I'll bear
Till death shall set me free,'

and by God's grace I've done it. I thank God for 'Little Piety.'"

"Amen!" said the colonel and the men.

THE HOSPITAL NURSE.

Loveliest of women! heaven is in thy soul,
Beauty and virtue shine forever round thee,
Brightening each other! thou art all divine.
—Addison.

When pain and anguish wring the brow,
A ministering angel thou.—Scott.

THE SURGEON rode up to the colonel's quarters, and hurriedly dismounting, put his bridle-rein into the hand of an orderly, and fairly ran into the room where the colonel sat at his desk. In a sort of breathless whisper he spoke one word—more dreaded by an officer who was responsible for a body of twelve hundred and forty-seven men than would be a battery of sixteen-pound napoleons, more terrible than any other to be uttered in the army—"Small-pox."

"Small-pox!" cried the colonel. "What do you mean? Where can it have come from? How—how—"

"Can't tell, Colonel, but there it is, and I don't know how it got so far before I found it out. It has just been reported to the hospital from one of the companies."

"What have you done with Mrs. Sinclair?" asked the colonel, as they looked blankly at each other.

"I have arranged that she shall not know it," answered the surgeon.

The regiment, which was a lately organized one, and of cavalry, was in quarters for instruction, equipment and the purchase of horses in a western town, and a school-house had been taken for a hospital. Of course, there were no wounded men there, but nearly every conceivable disease was represented; for though one would suppose that children's diseases were usually attended to, as they should be, in childhood, it was surprising that so many soldiers developed measles, chicken-pox, mumps, and all the ills that baby flesh is heir to, till one would think that never a child had been sick, and had recovered to grow up.

The nobility of our women was manifested during our war of the rebellion, not only in that they organized relief societies in every city and town and hamlet through the north for the rolling of bandages, and scraping of lint, and making of all sorts of necessary things for the men who were at the front, but in that they went into hospitals as nurses, and cared for the sick and wounded. No office was so loathsome or blood-curdling, by the sick-bed or where the catlin and saw were doing their awful work, but that they performed it with never a perceptible shrinking. Ah, wonderful women were the mothers and wives and sisters and daughters of our brave and self-denying volunteers!

Such was Mrs. Sinclair. Her young soldier husband had been shot dead in an early battle, and after her first wild grief she had put herself as nearly as she could into his place as a substitute; "if it could not be in the ranks," she said, to do what she could to keep the ranks full. The colonel had been a loved and trusted friend of that young couple since long before they were married—married only to be separated by the awful fiat of war—and she offered her services to him and for the hospital of his camp of instruction. So there she was, and now—the horror of the thought almost froze his blood—here was small-pox right by her, and she might be exposed to the awful disease which—he could not tell—was likely to number scores of victims before it was checked!

The colonel sprang upon his horse, and he and the good doctor fairly flew to the hospital. In the ward where lay the soldier all breaking out with the pustules of the loathsome small-pox, they beheld—horror of horrors!—Mrs. Sinclair kneeling by the side of the bed on which he lay, reading to him the beautiful prayers of the Church of England.

The tears started in the eyes of the colonel as he came upon the touching sight. She was so young, so beautiful, with the prospect of a long life before her, during which time might assuage the poignancy of her grief, and open to her the happiness that in this world does so often outlive the shocks of keenest sorrow:

But now she had taken the risk of a scarred and marred face that could never be overcome, but must be borne when the enthusiasm of patriotism had died out with its moving cause, and when regrets, keen and bitter, would but be added to the disfigurement. He thought of the days when he had carried her in his arms, a little child, and of her growth to the girlhood when she had been his pet of the household; of the deep feeling that showed in her eyes as she told her love for Harry, and that she was to consecrate her life to him, as she married him before he went to the service. He called to mind the awful day when he, the first major of the cavalry regiment in which her idol had commanded a company, had told her, as gently as he could, the sad, sad news that broke her heart, and he recalled the courage that yet bore her up as she said, "Half of me is gone, now I'll give the other half." Now was this the meaning, and was this to be the outcome of what he thought would be for her only a harmless occupation, by keeping her mind active while her hands were employed?—as, when he took the colonelcy of this new regiment, he had consented because she had so urged him to take her with him as nurse in the hospital of the camp of instruction. Her father was dead, and he had been a second father to her. Was this to be the tragic end of it all? His heart sunk within him.

"Hattie," he said, as he put his hand on her arm, "this is no place for you, my dear."

"It is just the place for me," she said, solemnly, and without looking up.

"Do you know what is the matter with this man, my child?"

"Yes, colonel, small-pox."

Then looking up into his face as she rose from her knees and stood before him, with her deep, brown eyes

"It is the man's place to take the brunt of war."

as full of light as those of an angel, and her face flashing out the love that filled her heart, she said:

"Why should he give his life, and not I mine? What is my beauty to me more than is his to him? Are the men the only patriots, and is not the country ours and calling for us as much as it does for our brothers?"

"Ah! but Hattie, it is the man's place to take the brunt of war; it always has been. You are not called upon for any such sacrifice. Let men, who can bear it better, take your place."

"My dear old friend," said she, "it is always woman's part to endure and suffer; and should not I do it for country, and for the men who are to so take the brunt of war? Christ died for the world—I may die for a little part of it. I can do that much, and, colonel, it is not so much as I have given already. This is the place for me, and here I shall stay."

"Did ever a land have such women?" said the colonel, as he walked away, and seeing to it that his lovely nurse was vaccinated, he left her to the care of the good God who watches over those who sacrifice themselves for others. She did not take the fell disease, and the surgeon said that her faithful and skillful nursing saved her small-pox patient to the service; but her consecrating sacrifice was just as great as if she had fallen a victim to it.

Yet she was but one of thousands of just such women in America, and they are the mothers of the Sons of Veterans to-day. What is the wonder that their sons and daughters make the Young People's Society of Christian Endeavor such a power, as they come to it with such a bravery and self-forgetfulness of consecration as they have inherited from the women of the war?

"YOU'LL BE SORRY FOR IT SOME DAY."

The work an unknown good man has done is like a vein of water flowing hidden underground, secretly making the ground green."—Carlyle.

I want to help you to grow as beautiful as God meant you to be when He thought of you first.—George McDonald.

Live as a part of the whole,
When thou art gone it remains.—Goethe.

HARLIE GRAVES was tough, there was no denying it, and tougher in sin than he was in sinew, which was saying a good deal, for he was a hard, daring rider, a perfect athlete, a dead shot, and the best with his sabre of any of the colonel's orderlies. Though the colonel had threatened to send him back to his company if he got drunk again, yet there he was at headquarters, for he was brave to recklessness, reliable—except that he would drink—and everybody knew he was devoted to his colonel.

One day, in a brisk little engagement, by an act of rare daring, he saved his colonel's life, but it was at the expense of a ghastly wound that he received. He merely said:

"Thank God I could a' done it, sir. I ain't no 'count; you be."

He had saved the life of the officer whom he idolized, though he knew nothing of that saying of "the Master," and which so often finds illustration in deeds of the rarest heroism:

"Greater love hath no man than this, that a man lay down his life for his friends."

In the hospital afterward, the colonel's eyes would moisten as he stood by Charlie's cot—for he wasn't killed outright—and found how deep a melancholy had settled over the poor fellow. He didn't swear any more, but he wouldn't talk, and seemed petulant if any one tried to find out what ailed him and made him so gloomy. Even the colonel couldn't get at the secret—for we all knew he had one—that troubled him so.

One day they moved some of the cots, and Charlie's was placed close to the door. The colonel came up very softly, so as not to awaken Charlie if he should be asleep, and found him lying with his back to the door. He listened to see whether the boy who had given his life for him was sleeping, and heard him say, all to himself:

"You'll be sorry for it some day, Charlie. O God! ain't I sorry for it!"

Then came a deep-drawn sigh that almost choked into a sob. The colonel went around to the other side of the cot, and, sitting down there, said:

He had saved the life of the officer.

"Now, Charlie, you must tell me all about it; it troubles you so much. You saved my life, my dear fellow, and it is little enough you will let me do in giving me this trouble to carry away from you. Tell me what you mean, Charlie. What is it you are sorry for?"

Charlie took the colonel's hand in both his as he lay there on the cot, and he half cried, he was so weak, as he said:

"You'll think it's a little thing, sir, for a man to be bothered about, but it's harried me for years, sir, and it's made me drink and be hard in trying to get rid of it by hazing as bad as ever I could, sir. I wanted to drown it out, sir, but it won't drown out."

"Tell me all about it, Charlie," said the colonel.

"When I was a boy in Sunday school, sir, way back in Massachusetts," said Charlie, "my teacher—he was a good man, sir, if there ever was one—was a talkin' to us about bein' Christians, and when he come to me I was sort of bored and mad-like, you know, and I swore at him in his talk. Then he looked at me kind o' sorry-like out of his big brown eyes—O God! I can see 'em now—and, sort o' gentle he says, says he:

"'You'll be sorry for it some day, Charlie. You'll be sorry for it some day.'"

Charlie choked up with his grief for a time, and then he said, in a despairing sort of way:

"He's been dead, my teacher has, these ten years, and ever since I heard he was dead, somehow that has seemed to come up all the time. When I go to sleep, I can see him again, and hear him say it just as he did then, a dozen years ago. And it's too late, sir; I can't take it back from him. O, there's no hope for me, sir!"

Charlie sank back on his little hospital pillow and covered his face with his hands for a minute, and then he said:

"Colonel, I've tried to get so drunk that I'd forget it, but I couldn't. And now, since I got hurt, if I get a little cat-nap of sleep, there I am back in the old class, the boys looking just as they used to, and the teacher looks at me, just so sorry, and says again, 'You'll be sorry for it some day, Charlie.' O, I can't stand it, sir; indeed I can't! That's what's the matter."

This last Charlie said in a sort of angry, desperate way, as though he was provoked. The colonel told Charlie, very kindly, that the teacher wasn't beyond his reach, but was at home with Jesus, and that when he prayed to the dear Lord and told Him his sorrow, he could get a double pardon from the teacher and Christ at once. Then he explained the lovely message that Christ left on the earth for just such as he, and pulled out a little Testament that he always carried, and read to Charlie from John 16:23, "Verily, verily, I say unto you, whatsoever ye shall ask the Father in my name, He will give it you." Charlie listened as if for dear life, and especially while the colonel was telling him why the "verily" was there. And then he said:

"Do you believe it, Colonel, just as it says?"

"Indeed I do, Charlie," said the colonel. "Try it, Charlie. Ask the dear Lord, and He'll do it. You can get it all wiped out. Why, a poor fellow, just dying on a cross by the side of Christ, called out to Him to forgive, and he did it." Then the colonel read the story of the thief on the cross.

Charlie lay still a little bit, and then, with his eyes shut, though tears were crowding through, he said:

"O Lord, I am sorry. I just am sorry. Oh, forgive it, and ask the teacher to forgive it." Then he waited a minute and said, "For Jesus' sake."

All at once he opened his eyes, and, looking up at the colonel in an anxious sort of a way, he said:

"Do you believe He heard it, sir? Do you think He done it?"

"I know He did," said the colonel, in a husky voice that was as full of tears as his eyes were.

Two or three days after, when the colonel went in, Charlie looked up in a happy way, and said:

"Oh, Colonel, I had another dream; I was in the class again. 'There,' thinks I, 'it's comin' again.' But the teacher looked at me, and says he, 'I'm so glad, Charlie!' Oh, sir, but it kind o' took a big load off."

Then he told the colonel how, all by himself, he had prayed, till finally he determined he would just trust it to the promise. Charlie didn't live long after that, but when we were standing about his peaceful cot, he said in a broken way, "It took a good while, sir, for the teacher's work to bring me round, but I believe he must have prayed over it, sir. And how is it that the verse reads with the 'Verily' in it?"

THE SOUTHERN DOMINIE.

Who builds a church to God, and not to Fame,
Will never mark the marble with his name.—Pope.

He was a man
Who stole the livery of the court of heaven
To serve the Devil in.   —Pollock.

We have just enough religion to make us hate, but not enough to make us love, one another.—Swift.

 TWO CLASSES of people in the South were a trial to us. They were those who claimed immunity on account of their defenselessness, and took advantage of it:—the women and the clergy.

The women we did not blame, for they suffered sorely. Their fathers, husbands, brothers and sons were gone to the war; they were left alone in the midst of armies on both sides that stripped and often burned their houses, ran off their horses and cattle, emptied their corn-ricks and spring-houses, appropriated their bacon and devoured their pigs and poultry; their slaves were emancipated or had run away; and they were "poverty-struck" and left with no way to turn. We bore their vituperation, when it came to us, as well as we could—but they were often adepts at it! Yet there were a good many noble exceptions to this.

But the clergy were another matter. Of course, as a general rule, they—that is, the better class of them —were Christian gentlemen, and we honored them. But there were exceptions, and we were treated by them in a most supercilious manner that was exceedingly offensive. "Endurance ceased to be a virtue," and we at last taught one of them a useful lesson, from which others wisely took the hint.

Colonel Topliff, who was commanding a cavalry brigade, was invited with his officers to attend divine service on a given Sunday—at a city church in the state, where his troops were operating, the pastor of which was a narrow-minded man,—and accepted. Accompanied by some sixty of his staff, field and line, he was shown into seats that had been set apart for them in the church, where they sat in a body; though no one spoke to them, save the usher who led them to the place assigned them.

Service went on as usual during the introductory part, though the "long prayer" was mainly devoted to the Confederacy, with a very earnest petition for Jefferson Davis and the success of the Southern arms; and the attending officers and the Union cause were naturally left out.

The sermon was on the theme of "original sin," as related to the then new theory of Professor Huxley's book on "Man's Place in Nature." In the course of it, the minister dwelt quite largely on what has since come to be known as the Darwinian theory, which he said was in a fair way to be exploded till recent developments had given it some fresh authority, as there really seemed to be manifestations of return to original type; and it could be seen illustrated throughout the city now in specimens of the ape tribe who were daily met on the streets, dressed in blue. The whole sermon was after this order, and with most barefaced insults hurled at the flag and the "Lincoln minions." The preacher was evidently hiding behind his sacred office and the house of God.

The Colonel whispered to one of his aids, who went out; but no further demonstration was made till after the benediction, when the people, as they undertook to leave the church, found crossed sabres at the doors, and a company of troopers drawn up in line before the church. The minister, pale, but with the look of one who courted martyrdom, came to the Colonel, and said:

"What does this mean, sir? Remove those guards and allow the people to go! Don't you know that this is the house of God?"

"You may find that it is also the gate of heaven," said the Colonel, "if you don't, as publicly as you have made them, retract the words you have spoken. I have detained the people that you may have the opportunity to withdraw your insult before all those who heard it. It was not an indignity to us, but to the Union. Take it all back before this congregation, and they may go."

"I'll die first!" said the minister.

"Though I said you might find it the gate to heaven," said the Colonel, "it is not really a matter of life and death, but of banishment. You will be sent through the lines this afternoon to find your heaven in the Southern army, while your property will be confiscated, sealed up and reported to Government, only to be restored to you on proof of your loyalty."

Some of his church officials told him they thought he had gone too far, and urged him to take it back and make an apology; but he was a very prominent Doctor of Divinity and a leading light in the southern branch of his denomination, and here was his opportunity to become a still greater celebrity and have his praises sung as a martyr all through the South. It was a chance for bloodless martyrdom, too; and, since no bodily danger was involved and he would be praised, féted and admired on all sides; and since he was sure that his property would not be harmed if it was put under seal, and would be restored to him when, if the war was disastrous to the South, he could recant, take the oath of loyalty, and come back into the Union, he remained obdurate.

So he was arrested, and in the afternoon, mounted on one of his own horses, was escorted beyond the lines by a squad of cavalry and turned adrift; solaced by the tearful looks of admiring women as he left the city. His house and stables and their contents were turned over to the proper Union officers, and nothing was harmed; though I understood that he had difficulty, even with the oath of loyalty which he grudgingly took, in getting all back again, if he ever did.

There are clergy, North and South, who are unworthy the high office which they have dared assume, and who bring endless reproaches on their churches and the religion which they profess to teach by their lives and words. They are a disgrace to their profession. Such an act as this which I have described snould be branded as rank cowardice, as much if committed by a Northern as by a Southern minister. There is no danger in it, since he is shielded by his cloth; and so there is no bravery:—and it is always mean to cast any "fling" from a pulpit, because it is a pulpit.

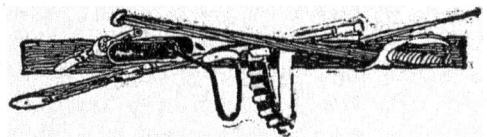

THE NORTHERN CHAPLAIN.

A gentleman born, Master Parson; who writes himself Armigero; in any bill, warrant, quittance or obligation, Armigero.—Merry Wives of Windsor. Act. I, Sc. 1.

See, a book of prayer in his hand;
True ornaments to a holy man.
—Richard III, Act. III, Sc. 7.

THERE were in the army Chaplains and Chaplains. The most of them were true and noble Christian men — both Catholic and Protestant. Their life was one of most self-denying labor, in camp and hospital; and such men were loved by the men and valued by the officers. Services were frequently held on Sunday, where the exigencies of the service would allow—often on the parade ground, where the men were brought up in close column of companies; and where the singing, with the aid of the regimental band, was enough to fire every heart; and the Chaplain could speak burning words of love and trust, with that appeal to loyalty and patriotism which made the men better soldiers.

But the main duties of the Chaplain were less prominent. He often acted as Postmaster, bearing letters to "the boys," that he might speak a tender and kindly word to them of home and heart; writing letters for poor fellows who could not write themselves,—and, strange as it may seem in our country of schools, there were many such; looking to remittances of money, after pay-day, to the dear ones left behind; conducting prayer-meetings with such as desired to attend them; and performing all the offices of kindness that a warm, human heart would prompt:—and daily visiting and comforting the poor fellows on hospital cots.

But once in a while there was a man who, finding no pulpit open to him at home, because of some moral defect that had become known, would, through political influence, secure a Chaplain's commission with its rank and pay of Captain of Cavalry, and be foisted upon a devoted regiment. Such ministers soon found their level; for keen eyes detected their tone, as the men missed their offices of kindness or saw through their thin veneer of piety.

Such a Chaplain succeeded in getting assigned to Colonel Nageley's regiment. He was a fine looking man and was cultured to a degree, so that he was socially welcome at the officers' quarters. But among the men he was a stranger, and no kindly word did they receive from him; as, standing on the dignity of his position on "the field," he maintained to them the hauteur of one who looked down upon them from his lofty height. Almost as much was he a stranger to the hospital of the regiment; never appearing at sick-call to see who needed his sacred words of comfort and cheer, and going among the sick only enough to keep up the semblance of his office.

He was often in the surgeon's quarters, to take a social glass with the officers, who were affected that way, and most of his time was spent in the Colonel's tent, where he smoked the good cigars he found there, played whist with the officers, told stories, and sang songs,— making himself very agreeable. But the Colonel was not blind to the interests of his regiment and the men he loved so well.

The matter seemed to come to a head when, after a stiff battle in which the whole regiment had been engaged, while the Colonel still commanded it and before he was assigned to brigade and the regiment was turned over to the Lieutenant-Colonel, he found that the Chaplain had been all the time back with the baggage train and out of reach of bullets.

As the Chaplain sat in his tent one day, smoking a cigar (to which he always coolly helped himself) the Colonel said, in his off-hand way:

"Chaplain, how are the boys getting on in hospital?"

"Oh; very well, sir, I think."

"How does Karl Ernest seem to you?"

"I think he is all right, sir; improving, I judge."

"Is he?" said the Colonel, fixing on him his stern, cold eyes. "I am very glad to hear it. I thought he was dead when I closed the poor fellow's eyes this afternoon."

"Is it possible, sir? Is he dead?" asked the Chaplain in some confusion.

"I thought so. But you should know better than I. That is your province rather than mine; though I try to see the poor fellows every day that I am in camp. I judge, perhaps, that you have not been at hospital to-day?"

"Well, no, sir; not to-day. I have been busy in camp."

"Have you been in hospital this week? I have not happened to meet you there."

"No, sir; I think not this week."

"Have you been there since we came to this camp, three weeks ago?"

"Oh, ye——"

"Think, Chaplain; you'd be apt to know if you have been in the new hospital."

"Well, sir, I don't know as I have;" and the Chaplain's face flushed with a sense of shame that he could not conceal; while fear showed itself in his eyes, as he furtively glanced at the Colonel whose stern eyes were fixed coldly upon him.

"Chaplain, we have not had service for several Sundays. Will you tell me why?"

"Oh, it's been so hot that I didn't like to have the men out under the broiling sun."

"But I told you some weeks ago that we would have the parade-ground policed over night, and have service before the sun got high."

"Yes, sir; but——"

"Chaplain," said the Colonel, interrupting him, "you don't seem burdened with duty, not even when the men are falling in battle; may be you have leisure to help me in some writing that I am anxious to have done. Are you willing to do me that favor?"

"Oh, yes, sir; I shall be delighted to do anything of the kind," said the Chaplain, evidently greatly relieved to feel that there was a way out of what in his heart he was cursing as a scrape.

"Then I'll be glad if you will go to the Adjutant's tent and write your resignation. I will send it up approved."

The poor, crestfallen Chaplain went out of the tent, and in half an hour the Adjutant brought the Colonel the paper he had asked for. It was sent up, duly approved, and came back accepted. When the Chaplain left, the boys gave three rousing cheers.

The Governor of the State from which the regiment came wrote to Colonel Nageley asking if he would accept a clergyman whom he named as Chaplain; and the Colonel replied that he would, if the Chaplain so appointed would pledge himself never knowingly to come within a hundred miles of the command.

THE PAY OF GLORY.

Oh, what a glory doth this world put on,
For him who, with a fervent heart goes forth,
Under the bright and glorious sky, and looks
On duties well performed and days well spent.
—Longfellow.

Oh, Fame! if ever I took delight in thy praises,
'Twas less for the sake of thy high-sounding phrases,
Than to see the bright eyes of the dear one discover
She thought that I was not unworthy to love her.
—Byron.

I.

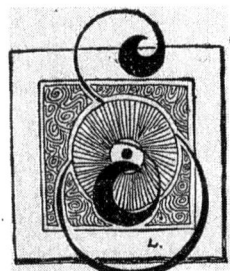
OON after the war—only a couple of years or so—a dear old comrade of mine was spending a few days with me. The memories of our bivouacs on the field led us to the throwing away of conventionalisms, as we sat together in my study after the family had retired, and called up the glorious past—the past par excellence—that lives in every soldier's memory. Way on into the evening, while the colonel took his meers-

chaum, we sat in the quiet of my study—my den—as he played over Goldsmith's Soldier:

> "The broken soldier kindly bade to stay,
> Sat by the fire and talked the night away;
> Wept o'er his wounds, or tales of sorrow done,
> Shouldered his crutch and showed how fields were won."

My friend's bedroom was close by my study, and that evening, after the tired wife had left us, he said:

"My limb pains me some to-night. You know how a foot-bath always relieved it. Let me get the little tub in here by the stove and sit with my feet in it while I blow my cloud. Then we can talk on."

So I brought it in and placed it where the glow of the fire came, and he rolled up his pantaloons and sat in a familiar kind of a way, calling up the different positions at Nashville when Hood was before it. His feet were enveloped in water and his head in smoke.

Just a few inches above his ankle, and showing a little below the edge of his rolled-up trousers, was the purplish brown edge of a horrid scar. I forgot what he was speaking of when I saw it. I was back beyond the Mississippi and beyond the latter years of the war, to the place and day when I saw that spot first. It was a ragged, ugly hole then, lined with the crimson flesh and quivering yet with the shock of the piercing minie. He was hopping on one leg, while his arms rested on the shoulders of two brawny men who loved their officer. The life blood was oozing from the wound, and yet he shouted, "Keep the men up!"

We sat together in my study.

I thought of a later day when I saw it again, and the edges showed the sickening color of the gangrene, while the atmosphere was filled with the odor of that dreadful aggravation which was brought by the heat of the southern hospital. He then said to me:

"It is humiliating that we are subject to such corruption, but, even when they are corrupt, we love our members, and I have told the surgeons that, bad as it is, I will defend my limb with my pistols, if need be, from the catlin and the saw."

So on this evening of which I am speaking I said: "Colonel, that ragged scar takes me back to Pea Ridge, and to the time when you were only a captain, and the memory is a holy one."

"Yes," said the colonel, bitterly, "I am one of thousands—officers and privates—who are in this fix. There was a time when we felt the glory, but it is so long ago. If I live to be a grandfather, little mouths may stand agape at my scars. But just now it seems like a cheap glory."

The colonel whiffed slowly at his pipe and then he said: "Now there was Hollingsworth, shot through the foot at Lexington. You remember he was made colonel of the —— regiment of —— infantry, and while yet a cripple from his unfortunate foot, he went with his command to the battle in which, with most of his officers, he was killed. Marshall, major of that regiment, had been a soldier for twenty-five years in the regular army, and he was shot with Hollingsworth. What I am at is this: two classes of glory are gained in two ways, one through brilliant service, and the other through long service; one with the intense pain of a bullet hole in the foot, and the other through the long-drawn pain of a quarter century of frontier life; and both immediately after promotion, end in death. Hollingsworth got his name mentioned in orders, and his face brought out in Harper's or Frank Leslie's or some of them; but who knows or cares about Marshall! Poor fellow!"

The colonel puffed vigorously at his meerschaum, and struck up a little tempest in the foot-bath by stamping in his earnestness, and then he said:

"Confound it! that is what bothers me. People say to me, when a twinge in my leg starts a grunt, 'It must be such a satisfaction to think how you got it!' That is just the thing I don't think of. I am only thinking how it hurts. Is it really an honor to one's manhood that he is to find comfort in the villainous aching of an old bullet wound, with the idea that he has not proved a coward? I'm not sure but one might better be a coward; and for that matter, it isn't proved, for just before I got this hole, I slid off my horse and stood behind him till I despised myself, and for very shame got back again. Whew! how the bullets flew. Now, what was that but cowardice?"

My old comrade sat quietly a few moments, and so did I, calling up the scenes of that day. All at once he said:

"Say, do you remember that chap of my company who was so nearsighted? You tried to wake him up after the battle was over, he lay dead so naturally. He has left a wife and children, and as they were married in the early days of Minnesota, when no records were kept, and afterwards moved to Illinois, the poor woman never could prove her marriage, and has no bounty nor pension yet.

"That leads me to the money idea of this sort of affliction. It is necessary enough to be sure; but how of the satisfaction? Think of a poor woman (there are plenty of them) toiling alone, having sacrificed everything in the world for her country, giving more than her husband did, for he only gave his life, and she has given the happiness of hers—with children to rear to—the Lord knows what! Somebody comes in and says to her: 'It is a comfort to think that your husband left such bounties and that the country gives such pensions!' How it must freeze up the poor heart that is left empty!

"People sometimes say to me, 'Why don't you take a pension?'

"Now, just think of the idea! I have a good income, enough for my necessities and to keep my meerschaum in operation; and, even if I hadn't, would you eke out glory with a remuneration for grunts over an aching leg? A grateful country, indeed!

"I fought all through the war, and long after the war was over I got a lame excuse for a lack of brevet and a request that I would give a history of my services, so that a brevet might be sent me, signed, probably, by President Johnson, when all the fighting I had done was under Lincoln, and that in answer to my own trumpet-blowing, placed on file, which might be resurrectionized by some great-grandchild some day, to the family chagrin!

"Pension, indeed! What if I'd been a quartermaster, what would the show have been?

"Now, there was Marshall, of whom I have spoken. Good, easy fellow, he was. You remember when he was at Clintonville—quartermaster of division. Well, he took me aside at St. Louis, and said, poor dog, that do his best, he didn't know what was to come! I'm not sure but it was a happy thing for him to close up his accounts as he did. But he was honest—thoroughly honest."

The colonel moved his foot about in the water, for his pipe was getting low, and said:

"I must go to bed, or your wife won't be in a pleasant humor toward me in the morning for keeping you up so late.

"Glory, indeed! It is a comfort to me that my limb aches less. But, ah! old boy, after all it was a glorious war, and a glorious victory, and slavery is done! Never mind—the hurt does pay!"

II.

In the morning, after breakfast, as we walked to the postoffice, I said: "Colonel, the glory of war may be, after all, in one's self. It is a satisfaction to think that one did his best, and he knows it, whatever may be the record outside. Glory may not be so much of a thing in the little way it comes to you and me—but we have our satisfaction."

"Yes, yes," said the colonel, "if one comes out all right. But glory is a back-hand sort of thing, after all. Here I'm limping as I walk. Now, what of it? I don't know but a limp is all well enough. There is Tom Gregory who limps, but one leg is shorter than the other, and has been from his childhood. Would I exchange limps with him? No. But why? My limp came to me in a glorious sort of way. When people look at him they say, 'Poor fellow!' When they look at me they don't say anything of the kind.

"Yet maybe I suffer more pain in a day than he does in a month.

"But where is my satisfaction? Is it in what people say, or refrain from saying? No! It may have no reference to what other people say or think, because I have the same feeling for myself that prompts them to look at me without pity. I don't pity myself.

"I don't quarrel with the glory—that is all well enough; but I do think that the satisfaction of that glory is a little slim at times. Take it, for instance, at a remove from the legitimate service.

"We were speaking last night of our old friend, Maj. Marshall. You recollect he had with him, at Clintonville, a little son—a boy of some dozen years—as bright a little chap as one often sees. One of the few officers who survived the horrid carnage of that regiment told me that the little fellow came on the field when his father fell (or was with him) and led his father's horse and his own pony off, with no regard to the raining of shot and shell.

"Now there was heroism—a heroism that in his life would have made his father's eyes snap with pride. But what of it all?

"The boy was not mustered in. Who reckoned his deed? What has become of him I do not know (I wish I did), but what of thousands of just such deeds by outsiders? The memory of them is in their own hearts, but in whose hearts besides where it can do them any good?"

Here the colonel stopped and put his hand on my shoulder and his voice grew deep as he said:

"My dear fellow, I am not a disappointed man in life, I have had my share of successes and of honors, but of this thing I am being every year more convinced: that the real glory of our acts, in war and peace, comes in the assurance we have of its being linked with the Eternal. My scars are valuable as they tell of a service that comes of principle. He who has no scars, but who fought under the leadership of a like principle, has a like glory.

"This fighting may be off from any smoky battle-field. A martyr is more than a hero. A man need not die to be a martyr. A sneer is harder to meet than a spherical case, or than a stake. No man with any spirit can stand too much blood mounting into his face. Noah standing sneers for a hundred and twenty years was one of the world's wonders. I always had a warm spot for Balaam. How could he endure it, poor fellow? Men fight duels because they can't bear a sneer.

"Death is a welcome friend if he covers one with his cloak from a sneer.

"Then he who stands for a principle in the face of a sneer is as great in the glory of his life as he who stands for a principle before a battery of napoleons.

"Here a man is finding a source of satisfaction within himself. He is getting a glory (soldier or civilian) that is to outlive the world, and is to be remembered by One who is at no loss for ways in which to turn it to account. Men may not understand a man's motives for a course of action. God does understand.

"The poor woman who gave her husband or son had no mortal reason for such a sacrifice but principle —she loved her country. If her husband or son was wounded or killed, there could be no glory for her. It was a killing sacrifice with no rebounding enthusiasm. The prayer that came with the sacrifice was a heart-prayer. The sacrifice reached far beyond earth, and was bound to Heaven.

"The satisfaction of this glory is to come in the life that is to be. It is a treasure laid up.

"Ah, my friend," here the colonel showed an emotion I had not seen before, "it is a comfort to me when I think that the real glory of our life work, growing out of our earth endurances, is not (and is not to be) a possession of the earth. It belongs to that land where 'moth and rust do not corrupt and thieves do not break through and steal.'

"You remember that ancient hymn:

> " 'Brief life is here our portion,
> Brief sorrow, short-lived care;
> The life that knows no ending,
> The tearless life is there.
> Reward of grace, how wondrous!
> Short toil—eternal rest!
> Oh, miracle of mercy,
> That rebels should be blest!' "

We had reached the house, returning from our walk, as the colonel closed the hymn, and he said no more.

While the colonel filled and lighted his meerschaum I couldn't resist the thought that he had hit upon the real philosophy of glory when he spoke of its onreaching.

Then its perpetuity must depend on the motive which actuated the man to become a soldier. Simple bravery was not enough. Heroic deeds would not secure it. The deep heart in the work, with an honest and pure motive—that was necessary.

A man might give himself to the war for a name, or for pay, or for any equally unworthy cause (of course this could not mean a private soldier) and the glory could not go beyond the present. But the love for country, linked with a love for the country's God—the two can hardly be divorced—being the motive, this can reach on and take hold on eternity.

What else can one see in the soldier's wife or mother? Where can there come in a selfish thought in her sacrifice if she is a true woman?

Even the poorest and most ignorant wife or widow of a soldier must come in for such a reckoning of honor, and God sees it as well as we. There is something holy to my mind about such people. They are heroines, and seem to be the ones whom we should hold in the highest honor.

There are the orphans of soldiers, too—blessed innocents, they have become the greatest sufferers, and the glory that they have in being the orphans of brave men has been bought at a dreadful sacrifice. Thank God that the country is waking up to its duty about them. They should be educated by the nation which has been saved at the cost of their orphanage, else their glory is the direst of all satires. So I thought on that morning, now so long ago.

III.

"We were sitting together in my study—the colonel and I—and, remembering our conversation of the morning, I said:

"One compensation of our service came in our leaves of absence and our final discharge. It is sometimes worth while to have the going away and the anxiety of the absence that we may enjoy the happiness of the return and reunion."

My comrade puffed at his pipe a few moments while he winked busily, and at last he said:

"There is another standpoint from which we need to look at this thing. It is one thing for a man to endure absence from home and the dangers of war, but he is occupied all the time. He is passing through danger, but he knows the danger and is not looking out for unpleasant news. It is quite another thing for the wife at home. She is not only robbed of her supporter and protector—the ivy robbed of its oak—but she is left, with nothing exciting to occupy her thoughts, in a state of anxious expectancy for dire news.

"The temporary separation may, by the chances of war, become permanent. Days grow long as they make weeks, and 'hope deferred maketh the heart sick.'"

"Well," I said, "this may come to the man as well. Now, there was Col. Dalton; you remember him,

It was a letter telling of the death of his wife.

Colonel; he got a letter just before the army started from Atlanta stating that his wife was ill and a little child of two weeks old was dead in the house. The doctor wrote the letter and said: 'Come home at all hazards if you would see your wife alive.' Dalton went to headquarters of brigade and found the general sitting on his camp-stool with his face buried in his hands. He broke in on the general's meditations with his grief and begged for a leave of absence. The general looked up with a haggard face, and pointing to an open letter on his mess-chest, said: 'Read that, Colonel.' It was a letter telling of the death of his wife and the orphanage of his children, who must be provided for. When the colonel had read it, the general said: 'I can't go, Colonel. I am bound by my oath to my duty, and dear as my children are to me, I am only one, even of this command of soldiers, who are worse off than we, and my family is but one of all the thousands of families that this war has reduced to such a plight! What do you think?'

"Dalton came back, almost broken-hearted. The next time he heard from home was after the command had reached the Atlantic."

"Was his wife dead?" asked the colonel.

"No," I said, "but it could make no difference in the fact of his having suffered during the whole march. Don't you recollect how gray Dalton got between Atlanta and the sea?"

The colonel nodded his head and then sat quietly for a time. Even his pipe went out as he sat so motionless. All at once he said:

"Dalton must have suffered. There are few of us who had families who can't remember just such experience in our history."

He winked for some time (he always winked fast when he thought) and at last he said quietly:

"Comrade, you can't measure even the horror of such an experience as Dalton's with that of a wife, who is withal the mother of a little dependent family, on getting word of a battle in which her husband took part, and after days of waiting, hearing that he is dead —or worse yet, badly wounded and she can't get at him.

"Let me illustrate the thing by an experience that I should speak of to no one else, and yet I don't suppose I have had it alone. You remember my own dear little wife?"

The colonel sort of choked up as he spoke. He seldom alluded to her. I did remember her—a sweet, clinging little sylph-like lady with a heart full of love. I know that the colonel's love for her was little short of worship. So I did not speak, but simply nodded— of course he knew I remembered her.

"About the time when my leave closed, just before our brigade left Nashville for Vicksburg and New Orleans, I sat at home and Jennie was sitting with me. I said:

"'Jennie, you are a heroine that you give up your husband so nobly. Talk of the women of '76!' So I tried to cheer her up. She said:

"'I am not going to cry—you shall see how brave I am. It is duty for you to go, then my duty is plain.

I did remember her.

You are not to go out of a rainstorm at home to find sunshine in the greetings of your regiment!' She gave an excited little laugh that I was fool enough to think was rather a light one.

"When I came to say 'good-bye,' she kissed me with a joke and laugh, and I was almost piqued to find that it seemed harder for me to keep tears back than for her. She kept waving her hand to me as long as I could see the house, and, like an old fool, I was almost provoked that she did not take my going more seriously.

"I got to the depot just too late for the train. There was no other till morning and I could do nothing but go home again.

"I found no one downstairs and went up to our room. There lay the little wife with her face in the pillow. I spoke to her, but got no answer. I took her up and she was senseless. I bathed her temples and tried to bring her back to consciousness. All at once she said, very sadly and dreamily:

"'That dreadful dream again. Alone! all alone! Oh, horrid war! Maybe he'll be killed—alone!—alone!' She kept saying it over and over again.

"All at once she seemed to realize that she was not on the bed, and turned to me with a little start as I held her in my arms. Then her eyes grew wild, and she shrank from me. 'My God!' she said, 'what have I done! O! I'm losing my mind! He—seems—to be—here—and I know—he's gone!'

"I pressed her to my heart and tried by caress and voice to make her understand that I was returned; but her mind had been overwrought through her effort at self-control, and she fell back fainting again. I laid her on the bed and summoned medical advice. The doctor gave something to produce sleep, and urged me to go and spare her another shock, as the real struggle of separation had gone by, and to repeat it might be dangerous. So I did not see her awake, and —I—"

I looked at the colonel. Great beads of sweat were standing on his forehead and the wrinkles were deep there.

I waited a few moments, and I said:

"You never saw her again, Colonel?"

"No," he said, and it seemed to choke him.

After awhile he continued:

"She got up from that and was well—lived for a number of months—and finally died very peacefully. But that was my last remembrance of her."

The colonel paced the room for some time, and then, as though rallying all his powers, said:

"I did not tell you this without a reason. It is to show how one woman suffered, and, if one, then thousands. This is the entail of glory. This is the detail —the inner make-up of what people call the glory of war.

"I may hold honor for my services, but what is that honor to me with this memory? Could I measure all the glory that men can give me against the life of that dear little woman? Sometimes when a person speaks to me of pride in view of distinguished service,

I feel ready to speak in a way that I should be very sorry to have spoken.

"But am I alone in this? No; there are thousands whose glory is just as empty as mine—just as empty.

"So there are thousands of patriot little women to whom the word 'glory' means just such suffering. Oh, but it is dreadful!"

We did not continue our talk that evening beyond this. Neither of us felt like it.

The colonel did not light his pipe again. When he had gone to his room, and I was alone in the study, I couldn't help saying to myself: "Talk of men who are heroes! The real heroes of the world may be found to be the women, with the heroism that comes of endurance—for it is harder to endure than to act."

The reserves, who stand in danger and wait, require more bravery than the advance who are in the thickest of the battle.

Milton Keynes UK
Ingram Content Group UK Ltd.
UKHW022146051224
3375UKWH00007B/337